FROM HOMELESS
AND HUNGRY TO WHOLENESS
AND HELPING

FROM HOMELESS AND HUNGRY

TO WHOLENESS AND HELPING

My Story of God's Redemption and Transformation

by Yvette Carter
as told to Jeannette (Wayman) Meitz

XULON PRESS

Xulon Press
2301 Lucien Way #415
Maitland, FL 32751
407.339.4217
www.xulonpress.com

Dedication

I dedicate this book to those who have believed in me.

First, to God who saved me.

To my husband, Michael, who has joined his life with mine. You have encouraged me to grow spiritually and helped me heal and begin to learn to trust.

To my children Peter, Robert, Claryvette, and Miguel (Miggie), to my sister Marissa, and my Mother – all who have forgiven me for my many mistakes that hurt them deeply.

To Mary Vaughn who believed in me and gave me hope when I didn't have any.

To Jeannette (Wayman) Meitz who encouraged me to write my story, having become my spiritual mentor, friend and confidante. God placed you and Frank in my life for a reason, beginning with the discipleship process several years ago.

There are so many others I could name who continue to be a source of encouragement in my life. Thank you! And thanks to God for all of you. I am truly blessed.

Yvette Carter

All proceeds from this book will benefit
VICTOR NEWMAN MINISTRIES

Victor Newman Ministries [a non-profit 501(c)3 ministry] is intentionally a coalition and network of organizations and servants committed to bringing the love of Christ to the last, the least, the lost, the left out and the looked over. We provide practical assistance to feed and house the homeless and rehabilitate those with addiction-related issues.

Our call is to see people saved, healed, set free, discipled, equipped, empowered and serving. Victor Newman Ministries was birthed to co-labor with God to facilitate His transforming lives from hopelessness into victorious new creations in Christ, and discipling (spiritually mentoring) them to spiritual maturity and fruitfulness, one life at a time.

For more information on VNM, or for an update on Yvette, visit our website: http://www.VictorNewman.org/.

vii

Never worry about numbers. Help one person at a time, and always start with the person nearest you.
– Mother Teresa

Then these righteous ones will reply,
"Lord, when did we ever see you hungry and feed you?
Or thirsty and give you something to drink? Or a stranger and
show you hospitality? Or naked and give you clothing?
When did we ever see you sick or in prison and visit you?"
And the King will say, "I tell you the truth,
when you did it to one of the least of these my brothers
and sisters, you were doing it to me!"
– Matthew 25:37-40 (NLT)

Table of Contents

Prologue

I *just got out of a relationship and have lost everything – my house, my job and my self-esteem. I have a son and daughter to care for, and that is the only thing that keeps me going. The other night, I noticed my son holding his stomach. I asked him what was wrong, and he said he was having hunger pangs. I knew immediately that things were much worse than I realized. I was going to have to find help if we were going to have a chance to survive, but I didn't know where to turn. How did I get here and what am I going to do?*

I came to the food pantry at St. Paul United Methodist Church in Largo, Florida, looking for help, because I was broken. . .broken to pieces. I was in a domestic violence relationship, and I didn't know how to get out of it. I asked myself, "What have I done to deserve what is happening to us? Lord, please forgive me for everything I've done, please. But I need you. I need to feel you near, because I can't do this alone." And at that moment I saw His presence, and that's where my story of redemption began.

This turning point in 2005 started me on my journey to where I am today: the Director of Open Arms Ministry, an outreach of

St. Paul United Methodist Church, where I had originally come seeking help to feed my family.

I am also President and CEO of Victor Newman Ministries, a network of generous givers and organizations working together to provide practical assistance to those who are broken, alienated and ostracized.

This is my story. I have made it this far only by God's grace, because He has my back. I know that today. No matter what anybody does, He's GOT me, and He chose me.

Whatever I do is for Him and for no one or anything else. If someone had pointed me to God earlier, I probably wouldn't have made so many bad choices. If I can give the clients at Open Arms just a little hope and faith, then maybe they won't make some of the same mistakes I've made. If it hadn't been for God, I don't know where I would be now. Maybe dead somewhere. Who knows?

Everything I have gone through – the domestic violence, the rape, the homelessness, not having enough to eat (being food-insecure), not having financial assistance, being in prison – was preparing me for His ministry, His purpose.

I pray that hearing my story gives you hope and you realize your tears and pain are seen by God, even though they may not be seen by the world. I want you to have hope and believe that it's going to get better, as you trust the Lord.

For those who want to be used by God to bring hope and healing to those in need and in pain, I want my story to show how to really help those who are struggling in similar situations. It's not about giving money; it's about listening and giving respect and words of encouragement to help them keep moving forward and finding salvation in the God who loves them.

Be sure to read the Epilogue (Chapter Eight) about what God is doing in my life at this very moment of writing my story. He is allowing me to experience illness, physical pain and struggle, but for His glory, I believe.

Most days I also write a devotional, "A Penny for Your Thoughts," and post online. I have selected 30 devotionals in Chapter Nine. Meditate on these a day at a time, as they aren't meant to be read in a hurry. I pray the scriptures and my words are helpful and inspirational as you seek God's best for your life, wherever you may be in your journey.

Blessings, Yvette Carter

CHAPTER ONE

The Beginning

was born in the Bronx, the oldest of six children. I didn't know my dad in the early years, and my stepfather didn't love me, because I wasn't his child. I felt like an "afterthought" since my younger siblings needed more of my mother's care and attention, not leaving much left over for me. I wasn't sure back then that she really loved me, but felt she probably did.

All my life I thought I was ugly. When I was very young I was told I had a big nose. I used to bite my nails. I didn't have many friends. So my self-esteem was shot from childhood. You see, what parents say to a child has tremendous impact to harm, or to help. So I grew up thinking that all the girls were prettier and smarter than me. I didn't know why I was born. I didn't have any future. I just kept on making mistakes.

Even my grandmother never loved me. I never knew why. I felt I was always just the "side-kick," the one who talked too much at home. In school, I remember not having many friends and feeling that no one really wanted to talk with me. All those feelings of insecurity contributed to the mistakes I made, going to the streets looking for people to love me. Little did I know that at that time God loved me anyway, but because I didn't have a relationship with Him, I didn't know that.

I met my real dad when I was 13. I wanted him to like and love me, but I don't believe he did, because I wasn't pretty enough. He would complain that I had too much acne and ask me why I wasn't taking care of myself. He was very critical of me. I saw my father treat my cousins well because they had blond hair and blue eyes. Every time I saw him, he just handed me money or a shirt or something. That's not what I really wanted. What I really wanted and needed was a father.

When my biological father started coming around to visit me, my relationship with my stepfather got worse. That's when the abuse really started. For more than 10 years I was abused a

My First Communion

lot by my stepfather. Because of this, I was always looking for acceptance and for someone to love me. So I have struggled a lot.

My mother forced me to go to religious instruction in the Catholic Church. I had my first communion, but I didn't really understand it. I knew about God, but I didn't really know Him. I believed that if I did anything wrong, I would go to hell. We didn't regularly go to Mass as a family, but I would often attend church just to get out of the house. I didn't have a personal relationship with God or know that I could be forgiven.

2

At age 17 I ran away from home and began "running the streets." By that, I mean I was partying and running wild, doing anything and everything that I wanted with no consideration for others or potential consequences.

Before long I met the man who would become my two oldest children's father. He was older and offered me "love" and money, both things I couldn't get enough of at home. I was very naïve and vulnerable. He lured me, and I fell for it. I didn't understand what was happening. I have replayed it in my mind many times and understand now how he did it. Because I didn't have a support system at home, I tumbled straight into his open arms.

I realized he dealt drugs when I was pregnant with my first child, Peter. But all I thought about then was getting "things," because I never had them growing up. I thought it was cool. I used to travel, had the finest clothes and best jewelry, but it all came with a price.

He went to jail the first time when Peter was one year old. I had no money, because he also had a drug habit and didn't leave anything for me to survive on.

He was in prison for three years. I can see now that God was giving me an opportunity to get out of that relationship, but I went back to him when he was released. You see, more people were expecting "street behavior" from me than giving encouragement or asking, "What are you doing?" I didn't know what else to do.

PRISON

When he came home from prison, he started dealing drugs again, escalating to the big time stuff and was arrested again. This time I was arrested, too, for being with him. I didn't want to turn state's evidence and testify against him. (I had learned and,

3

therefore, followed the "code of the street.") I went to prison, too, at the age of 21. He was sentenced to 25 years. I was sentenced to six years to life. I did six years.

I had to leave my two sons with my mother. Peter was now five, and Robert was only a month old. When they took me away, I remember Peter grabbed my leg and wouldn't let go. That image haunts me to this day.

My mother suffered dearly when I went to prison. She had to take care of Robert, my newborn, who was asthmatic. She also had to work. Because I was gone, Peter was disobedient in school. He was upset and lashed out at people. So she had to cope with my mess.

We think we are the only ones who have to deal with the messes we make. I learned that isn't true. Often, other people have to clean them up.

I know now my mother loves me because I am her child, just like God loves us because we are His children. Not only was she carrying her own burdens, she had to take on my load of responsibilities. In addition to her own children, she raised my two boys for six years.

I saw my sons only through prison visitations. I have a great deal of pain because of this. Robert didn't know me and wouldn't come to me during these visits, since he was so young when I was sentenced.

I now tell parents that the mistakes we make follow us, so think about the consequences of the choices you make.

The other person who suffered a lot when I was arrested was my 10-year-old sister, Marissa. I had practically raised her. She would follow me everywhere and often stayed with me on weekends and holidays after I left home. She was five when Peter was born, and enjoyed helping me care for him. Marissa was in court when I was sentenced. I remember it like it was yesterday. I was sentenced and immediately whisked away to prison. I wasn't allowed to hug her or say good-bye. She left screaming and crying, totally inconsolable.

Prison is another world. It's a jungle where you have to struggle to survive, to stay alive, or you will get raped and abused. I recognize now that God was in prison with me, regardless of my choices. Otherwise, I would never have survived those six years. I had to fight a lot to protect myself. I almost got raped. I was in solitary confinement for 90 days because I had to beat up someone to protect myself. I didn't know what would happen from day to day.

Prisoners are allowed to attend church services, but sometimes inmates go to church just to get out of their cells. I didn't want to do that. I didn't want to go just for that reason, so I did not develop a relationship with God in prison.

I thanked the Lord when at 27 I came home from prison, but even then I didn't change or develop a relationship with Him. I failed to allow God to change me.

I had just gotten out of prison

5

I came home to the Bronx and started working as a manager in a company, making $40,000 a year. Then I met the man who would become the father of my two youngest children, Claryvette and Miggie. He also was dealing drugs.

Even though God had blessed me with enough income to stay out of the street life, it wasn't enough for me. I wanted more stuff. I was paying all the bills without any help from him.

After a while he went to the Dominican Republic, supposedly to build us a house. I sent $600 a week to him for over a year to help with the construction. He found someone else there, and never came back. He never repaid me the money I had sent. I lost everything.

God was telling me "change your ways; change your thinking; change your heart." If you just change your ways, your behavior, you are still the same person inside. You have to let God change your heart, because it starts from the inside out. You can't change just the outside, the appearance, but that is what I was trying to do. I didn't listen to what God was speaking to my heart.

I was still living in New York with my younger two children (Claryvette and Miggie). Peter and Robert were living in Florida with my mother, because they didn't get along with my younger children's father. I had one foot in the streets and one at home. I had no money. I had nothing. So I went back to the streets. I started dealing drugs. It was the only way I knew how to survive. I didn't know what else to do.

Yvette and Claryvette in New York

Yvette and Claryvette in 2012

MOVING TO FLORIDA

One day I was thinking about my youngest children, and I realized that I couldn't continue like this. I didn't want to end up back in prison, so I decided to move to Florida. With about $7,000 I came to stay with my mother until I could find a job and get a place to live and buy a car.

Then I met another guy in Florida, that later turned into a domestic violence relationship. I was 33 or 34 when I moved to Florida, thinking things would get better. But no, it didn't get better, because I hadn't allowed God to change my heart.

Little did I know that this relationship would turn out to be the worst. He smoked weed and often punched me. It was like I was attracting the wrong people. I was making bad choices. I thought I wasn't worthy. I settled. I thought I wasn't good enough. My self-esteem was on the floor. I was always told I wouldn't amount to anything and that I would always go back to the streets. And rightly so – because I had always gone back before.

The abuse escalated after I brought all my belongings from storage in New York. I had beautiful furniture, clothing and "things." I was living in my own place, a duplex, with my two youngest children.

He was beating me up. Still I made wrong choices, because I had no one to tell me that I didn't have to put up with him and what he was doing to me.

I had finished collecting unemployment from New York State and wasn't working, so I couldn't pay the rent. After that, I lost everything – my car, the furniture – everything. Everything that I lost, though, I had bought with drug money, dirty money.

Even after everything was taken away, I was able to get into another smaller place. He was also living with us, and the beatings intensified. Wrong choices. I made a LOT of bad choices. I thought I wasn't pretty enough. I wasn't smart enough. I didn't speak right. So I settled. If I would have known that I am made in God's image and am beautiful in His eyes, it would have made a huge difference. But I didn't know that then.

I still struggle with self-image. But now I have what money cannot buy. I have His love, His grace, and I carry Him in my heart, which cannot be taken from me. What God has done, no one can do.

I decided to try church, but when I did, people just looked at me, judging. Sometimes you go to church because you need someone to encourage you, not to judge you. I felt shame. I felt everything was my fault. I said, "Oh God, I come to church and these people don't care."

My passion to help the homeless and hungry comes from these experiences. I don't want people to come to our church or to the food pantry and think that we don't care. That's what drives me to do what I do.

Sometimes when we are going through difficult times, there is no one in our circle to say, "It's going to get better. You just have to trust God." They either give you wrong advice or they judge you, or just ignore you.

When you ask people, "How are you doing?" you need to be prepared to listen –to really listen. Otherwise, if you just want to hear "fine," then don't ask. Don't ask "How are you doing?" and just keep on walking. Many times that happened to me.

I left that church, because I felt more shame there than I did in the streets.

CHAPTER TWO

Healing Begins

My stepfather was dying. I went to the Moffitt Cancer Center (in Florida) every day to take care of him, because my mother had to work.

He had abused me when I was young, and I knew that he didn't love me because I was another man's daughter.

At this time, I was slowly beginning to attend another church. He would call me Mother Theresa. I would get offended, because I didn't know why he called me that, but God was showing him qualities in me that I could not see yet. He realized I wasn't all that bad and also that the things he had done to me were wrong.

Then he asked for forgiveness for everything he had done that had hurt me and expressed that he loved me. I just smiled and told him that I loved him, too, and not to worry – that we were okay. Later I really forgave him on his death bed.

I just wish he had shown me appropriate love when I was young, although it was helpful to find out that he regretted abusing me. When you are a child and you don't feel loved, you turn to the wrong people searching for someone to love you. Those wrong people often take advantage of you, because you have low self-esteem and are so vulnerable.

And that's what happened to me. I don't blame anyone for my mistakes, because they were my choices. However, it would have been helpful for him to show appropriate fatherly love to me when I was a child.

Little did I know that was the beginning of the healing process for me. It was the beginning of the journey that would lead me to serve the Lord.

DOMESTIC VIOLENCE

One day I came home from visiting my stepfather at the hospital. The man I was living with asked "Where were you?"

When I told him, he punched me right in my mouth because he didn't believe me. He was on drugs and hallucinating.

I fell, and then ran out to the garage and threw myself on the floor. I cried out, "God, whatever I've done, I am so sorry. I am even sorry for dealing drugs. I know that those drugs were killing your children. I am so sorry, and I need you to help me." I still regret dealing drugs, with all of my heart.

In that moment something happened. I am confident that God was directing things, because the police showed up and arrested him. I didn't call them; I didn't have a phone. They had a warrant for his arrest for something else.

When they saw my bruises, they asked questions and pursued the obvious circumstances a little further. Later when we went to court, God gave me the courage to get an injunction for life against him to never come near me.

My two youngest children were living with me at that time. I am thankful that he never hit them. I was fearful for my life, but God helped me.

MY FIRST VISIT TO ST. PAUL

Then, because I had no food or money and two hungry children, I came to St. Paul United Methodist Church in Largo, Florida, to ask for help. They had just a small pantry in the front office.

I walked in and said, "I need some food."

Miss Mary Vaughn, the Office Administrator, looked at me and asked, "Do you want to volunteer?" I didn't want to look at her, because I was ashamed and bruised with several teeth missing, and I still didn't trust church people.

I said, "Ma'am, I am not here for that. I am begging you for food. I have two children. They don't have food. Please. Please." So she gave me the food.

She said, "If you ever want to volunteer, come back."

One morning I felt compelled to go back to the food pantry. I didn't have a car because I had lost everything, so I walked. It must have been about 15 blocks.

When I got there, Miss Mary saw me – and before I could even speak – she said, "You're here to volunteer. I'll call Shaun."

Shaun Powers, the Worship Leader with staff responsibility over the homeless ministry, came and said, "I'm so glad you have come to volunteer." I still hadn't spoken a word, and I wouldn't look at either of them directly.

They took me to the 16' x 16' pantry room, with clothes piled all over the place. It was a mess. He said, "You can start here, and do whatever you think; whatever you are led to do." I didn't really understand what he was saying. But I replied, "Okay."

I started sorting and folding clothes. Then I felt God speak to me. I started crying. I said, "God brought me here to clean the mess here in His house, while He started cleaning the mess in MY house." And, of course, Miss Mary gave me the food I needed for my children.

I began to walk to the church twice a week to help in the pantry room, and they would give me food. In time, I started coming to help two hours every day. Then something happened and I started to arrive at 8:30 am and not leave until 5:00 pm EVERY DAY. That was in 2009.

As I sorted and folded clothes and cleaned that small room, a peace would come over me. When Miss Mary came to see how I was doing, it was all organized. I don't know how I did it, but I did!

I didn't know about the Holy Spirit then. I didn't know what was happening. I just knew I wanted to spend more time there, because that's where I found peace. I was there with God. I know it today, but I didn't understand it then.

I would go to the church pantry while Miggie (my youngest child) was in school. It got to a point where my coming wasn't negotiable. This is where I needed and wanted to be. That's the bottom line.

And that's how I started to get involved in this ministry of helping others. I said, "Oh God, I don't know what to do here." But as time went on, God grew the ministry. It's like I am the pencil, but God does the writing. Everything He has written I have followed to the best of my ability.

OPEN ARMS MINISTRY

They eventually gave me the keys to the one-room pantry. I was still just getting on my feet. My youngest son was in school, and we lived in a small place. We didn't have much. I didn't have a paying job and was surviving on disability payments and food from the pantry. (I have migraine headaches because of the beatings, as well as gout and osteoarthritis.)

In November, 2009, I was significantly struggling financially and was about to lose my car. St. Paul helped me pay the back car payments, so I could drive to Open Arms.

In church staff meetings I wouldn't speak. I didn't feel like I belonged there. I felt unworthy and out of place.

I often felt overlooked and unappreciated. It took a lot for me not to leave. I wanted to, but God wouldn't let me. He told me just to wait. He had put me there for a reason. I didn't work in the ministry for recognition or acceptance. God advocated for me.

I also felt out of place because I didn't go to college or have a degree in food distribution. Then God began to show me that I HAD studied it, because I had LIVED it! I didn't need formal education to do what He wanted me to do. Everything I had gone through – the domestic violence, the rape, the homelessness, not having enough to eat, not having financial assistance – was preparing me for His ministry, His purpose. That was my education! When I doubted, He gave me confirmation. When I was blind, He gave me sight. When I couldn't speak, He gave me His words.

Each thing I do today to help the community is because I lived it, and God helped me learn and understand that I was never alone, no matter who rejected me. God didn't reject me. I learned to look at myself through God's eyes – not through other people's eyes, trying to be someone I was not.

I also didn't feel like I fit in at church – it was such a big church. I wasn't dressed like everyone else. People criticized and judged me because of how I dressed, and because I was the only Hispanic.

After about a year and a half, the church moved the pantry across the street to a house owned by the church, and the ministry became known as Open Arms.

SALVATION

In April of 2010, I completely gave my life to the Lord. I continued working at Open Arms. I started more faithfully attending church at St. Paul UMC, and I was baptized.

Then I got more deeply into God's Word. I went to Bible studies led by Shaun Powers. If I didn't understand what we were studying, I wouldn't ask questions because I was so embarrassed. I would wait until everyone left, and then I would ask Shaun to explain the Bible verses to me.

I didn't have the knowledge that I have today. Shaun had faith in me when I didn't have faith in myself. I didn't yet have a deep relationship with God. Shaun helped my spiritual growth a lot during this time. I also completed training to become a Stephen Minister, since I wanted to do outreach ministry.

Good things started happening at Open Arms. The ministry was growing, and we were serving more people.

FAMILY HEALING

When I went to prison, my middle son, Robert, was one month old. When I came home, he was six years old, going on seven. He grew up hating me. He said I didn't love him. He was always jealous. He said I was a slut, that I was nothing. He felt and said these things, because he believed that I should have been more responsible and taken care of him. He was right.

In 2012 when Robert was 30, God turned his heart around, so that he could forgive me.

No matter how much I told him I loved him, he didn't believe it. He just judged me and judged me. It's really hard to have a child tell you they don't love you; that you were a bad parent; that "you messed up my life because you weren't there."

I cried every night, because I didn't know how to fix our relationship. I cried out to the Lord, "I don't know how to fix this. I need your help."

Then one day Robert called me a "bitch." I wanted to wring his neck. At this point, though, I was on God's path and beginning to see things through His eyes. I thought about when Jesus was on the cross, and he looked at the people and said, "Forgive them for they know not what they do."

I knew this boy was so broken, but I didn't know what to do. I prayed, and God directed me to knock on his front door one morning at 7:00 am.

I told Robert, "I love you. I am so sorry for what I made you go through. I really am. I have asked you time and time again to forgive me. I am sorry I am not the mother you wanted me to be. But today I am becoming who God has created me to be. And I am asking you to forgive me. You don't have to love me if you don't want to. I understand, because I messed up. I was naïve and stupid. And you're right. I wasn't thinking about you." I told him details he didn't know, and that helped his healing process, as well.

That boy cried and cried and cried. From then on his whole attitude changed, because now he has seen that no matter what he's done or what he says, I am available, loving him and accepting him.

Robert has a son, Antonio. The relationship I didn't have with Robert because I was in prison when he was little, I have gotten with Antonio. He has gotten attached to me. It's like everything I wanted to do for Robert but couldn't because I was in prison, I get to do for Antonio. It's as if God has given me a double blessing. He has healed my relationship with Robert, and has given me the love that I missed when I was away from Robert.

With Robert's son, Antonio

God says that when you are following His path that your family members may not be behind you. But as you continue, they will follow. They will. Robert has seen the changes in my life.

I thank the Lord that He healed my relationships with all four of my children. It took a lot of work and patience and grace. Sometimes you have to go through the pain to get the healing. I learned that, but it was worth it, since I have good relationships with all of them today.

All four of my children now work with me in the ministry of Open Arms. I am blessed.

My four children: Peter, Robert, Claryvette, Miguel

Sometimes you have to ask for forgiveness and not try to justify your actions, because of what you did. You did it. Don't justify what you have done or try to explain it away when you were wrong. Don't blame other people. You must take responsibility for your own actions and the people you have hurt. God helps you with that and with the shame. That's what He did for me.

Do you know how it feels to say to your child, "I know I messed up as a mother?" That's hard. That's really hard. You never want to admit to your children that you screwed up. But it had to be said. And the healed relationships are worth the work.

I have hurt a lot of people, which means I have had to ask for forgiveness a lot. In 2013 God helped me realize how much I had hurt my sister, Marissa. When I asked forgiveness for everything I had put her through and told her I was sorry for hurting her, she

replied that she loved me anyway and didn't judge me. I needed
to acknowledge that I had hurt her, however, for my own growth
and healing.

Today my mother and
I have a great relationship.
She has forgiven me for
my disobedience. Seeing
the transformation in me
has changed her, because
she couldn't believe I
would ever change. For her

Yvette with mother, Carmen

to see me where I am today, and be part of the ministry at Open
Arms, has changed her thinking about me – and that is huge.

In the past six years that she has been doing ministry with
me, she has also learned to forgive and be forgiven. She used to
be very bitter. She hated Peter's father for what he did to me. But
I accepted my responsibility in the relationship and explained
that no one makes us do anything. I couldn't let her blame him,
because I had a choice in those decisions. I asked her for forgiveness because I made her suffer so much.

The older boys' father died in 2016. Before he died, he told
me, "I am so sorry for ruining your life. I need to ask you for
forgiveness because I was an adult, and you were a child. But I let
my lust take over. I am so sorry."

This was very hard. Although I had sort of forgiven him
before, it had been for the wrong reasons. This time, I forgave him
to let him move forward, so God could help him forgive himself.

This time I responded, "I forgive you. Yes, I was naïve, but
there was a time I could have made different decisions, but I

didn't. I can't put all the blame on you. I have to accept that my choices were also wrong."

I had to step out of my denial and quit blaming other people for my decisions. God will help you see that if someone is asking for forgiveness and you don't forgive them, then you are also part of the problem.

Robert hated his father. Hated him because of the way he was, what happened to me and, therefore, what happened to him. I told Robert, "Your father is dying and you need to talk to this man."

He said, "I will not. I hate him."

I said, "God forgives us for the things we have done. Have you ever offended anyone? Have you been forgiven?"

He said "I have."

So I asked, "Why won't you give forgiveness, as God has forgiven you?"

"I'll think about it," was all he said.

I prayed, prayed, and prayed on it. Robert finally called his father in the hospital via Skype, allowing them to see each other. His father then asked for forgiveness.

Robert told him, "Dad, I've always loved you. I was just mad because you were never there. But I love you, and I forgive you. You can be at peace because I do love you."

Two hours later, Robert's father died.

Afterwards, Robert called me crying, "I am so thankful that you insisted I call my father." And that allowed him to begin to heal, as well.

Now it is up to Robert to cut the chain and not take all that bitterness and anger to his family.

**Robert's family: L to R: Bella, Miah, Antonio, Jeremiah,
Robert holding baby Noah**

We have a choice to change, to tear off that chain of bondage. We don't have to continue doing what our parents did. The mistakes we make, we pay the price – and so do our children.

The mistakes done to YOU, also have a price. It's like a chain reaction. I've learned that we have a price to pay, just like Jesus did. He paid the price for our sins, but we also pay the price. We have consequences for what we've done. Only God can make our hearts right with Him.

I know today that God is using everything I went through to help others and spread the Good News. He also enabled me to break that chain – to change my ways – not to carry it to the next generation.

Feeling unloved by my parents and my grandmother probably happened because my grandmother's parents didn't show her love. She continued the same pattern with her daughter. My mother took it to us with the same damaging results.

The chain of abuse, neglect and other sins has to be broken. Most people don't know how to do that on their own. Only God can do that. Only God can help us to forgive and change and fill that deep void in our hearts.

CHAPTER THREE

Getting Married and Becoming a Pastor's Wife

GETTING MARRIED – FOR THE FIRST TIME

I used to go to Celebrate Recovery at St. Paul, which was meeting at Open Arms. It's for hurts, habits, and hang-ups. I didn't have drug issues then, but I did have hurts – plenty of them.

So I started going to meetings, and that's where I met my husband, Michael. Although I saw him there, I wasn't looking for a man. I had no interest. My focus was only on the Lord, bottom line. I didn't want to be bothered with another relationship.

Michael has since told me that he would watch me, but I don't remember, because I didn't flirt. I was just paying attention to God and what He was saying to me.

After about a year of attending Celebrate Recovery, I received a message from an unknown number: "Do you feed people who are hungry?" I texted back, "Who is this?" He didn't respond.

Then I received another text, "Can I stop by for lunch?"

So I told my Celebrate Recovery leader, who is a Parole Officer for Pinellas County, "Mr. T, somebody is texting me, and I don't know who it is." He checked the number and told me, "Yvette, that's Michael."

I replied, "Michael, who?" and he said, "Michael Carter. Do you want me to tell him to stop?" I told him no. He hadn't said anything offensive; I just wanted to know who was texting me.

Finally I trapped Michael into talking to me by calling from my office rather than my cell phone, and he picked up. I said, "I know who you are." And I hung up.

Yvette and Michael when first met, November 2011

In November of 2011 Michael again texted and asked if I wanted to go for coffee. I didn't know if I should, so I prayed for guidance from the Lord, because I didn't want to make another relationship mistake.

I went, and when I asked him what he wanted, he said, "I want to get to know you."

I replied, "Mr. Carter, if you are a womanizer, I don't want to be bothered. Please leave me alone. Please." That's how our relationship started.

We began seeing each other regularly and got engaged in February, 2012. I had told him I wanted a big wedding since I had never been married, and we had agreed that we would get married in a year, so we could plan the wedding.

I prayed, "Lord, you have placed me in this man's life for a purpose. I don't know what it is, and I don't know what you want me to do, God. All I am asking: please do not let him get in my path, if it isn't for good. That's all I ask. I don't ask for money, for wealth. I just can't go through another damaging relationship."

Then in May Michael shocked me. "Let's go to the court house and get our marriage license." Two weeks later he said, "Let's get married tomorrow! Pastor David will marry us."

So we were married on May 12, 2012 – just the two of us and Pastor David and two witnesses from St. Paul.

Yvette and Michael's wedding. May 12, 2012

25

And that's how two broken people from different situations came together. God knew that we could minister together because of our pasts.

It's been challenging working through a marriage relationship after all that we individually have been through, even though we love each other with the love of the Lord. No marriage is perfect. However, God made us perfect for each other. Michael has been an encouragement in my life. . .and a mirror.

God is the foundation of our marriage, and He knew what He was doing when He put us together. As time has gone by, our love has grown and the foundation has gotten stronger, even when we don't agree. We walk side-by-side in our marriage and ministry, because God has asked us to do it together. We both came with rough edges, but from the beginning God was smoothing our edges, so that we fit better together.

I believe in my husband and trust him to the Lord, as he must do with me. God is using us to help each other, and others, as we continue to become the people that God created us to be.

We know that God has a plan for our marriage and our lives. But I have learned that we are all broken, and it's a process. Some of us have more to heal from than others and more things to let go of.

Sometimes it's hard for me to believe I am worthy, not only of God's love, but also of the love of my husband. I still struggle with feelings of insecurity and also have trust issues because of all I have been through. While the Lord is helping me with that, it will probably be a life-long challenge.

Yvette and Michael in May 2016 at the beach

TRANSFORMATION CONTINUES

While it wasn't easy, the transformation I went through was by the power of God working in and through my thoughts, emotions, words and actions. I would have moments of absolute elation as I was going through this process, and also moments of sheer terror. I often asked God "What are you doing?" I had broken out of the box of conformity that said, "Don't; don't; don't."

In my heart the Spirit of God was saying, "It's okay." I embraced the bright and beautiful future to which God was calling me.

When I started reading the Bible, I claimed not to understand it. However, I didn't want to hear and put into practice what I did understand! I was taking baby steps.

The Bible speaks to us about how we should live our lives. We tend to read it, believe, and ask for forgiveness but then don't give up the sin. Yes, God forgives, but if you keep on reading, He says "Go and sin no more." Don't keep doing it again. I had to let God work on the roots of my heart and the deep hurts from the past.

In 2013 I went through a discipleship class using the DTI materials (Discipler Training International, available at no charge at www.Disciplers.org). I still have the book from the class with all my notes.

While the weeks under Frank Meitz's facilitation were invaluable, one major concept really made a difference and is engraved on my heart.

We discussed the analogy of our lives being depicted as a house with different rooms, representing different areas of our lives. When I became a Christian, I invited Jesus into my house (life) only as a "guest." But I realized through this exercise that He has ownership of the entire house (by what He did on the cross), and doesn't want to just live in my guest room and my spiritual room. No, God wants all of you or nothing. He won't force you, but He isn't going to settle for just living in part of your "house."

While both resources are invaluable, DTI is different than Celebrate Recovery which is about hurts, habits, and hang-ups, where a sponsor serves as an accountability partner. DTI promotes having a spiritual mentor come along side you to share the principles of inward transformation, Lordship and Abiding with scripturally-based materials. (Jeannette Meitz has been one of my spiritual mentors.)

I constantly speak to the Lord, because that's my sanity. I go to Him for everything. I refuse to do anything without the guidance of the Lord because when I do anything without His consent, I make mistakes. When I think I can do it on my own is when I get into trouble.

With Frank and Jeannette Meitz from Discipler Training Int'l

BECOMING A PASTOR'S WIFE

I didn't marry a preacher. God called Michael to become a pastor several years after we got married.

When Pastor David was appointed to a different church in 2015, Michael became the pastor at Lake Palms Community Church, a Free Methodist congregation, later leading them through the merger to become Crosspointe Community Church.

And that's how I became a pastor's wife. Did I think I would ever be a pastor's wife? Absolutely not! That was the furthest thing from my mind! It is also a lonely place. It is hard dealing not only with the members, but also with what they are saying about my husband or what he is going through. It's not easy. But my love for the Lord and my husband is so strong that I just say, "Okay, Lord. Please help me forgive them. I know you have forgiven me, so I must forgive them."

**Lake Palms Free Methodist Church praying for Michael & Yvette
on Pastor Appreciation Sunday**

Now God has led us into additional ministry together in a new non-profit (501(c)3) venture: Victor Newman Ministries. We believe God will continue to work through us to bring even more healing and restoration through this new adventure.

NOTE: For more information on Victor Newman Ministries, visit our website: http://www.VictorNewman.org/.

CHAPTER FOUR

Being Homeless and Hungry

H ave you ever been homeless and hungry? I have. . . .several times. Life was not easy, but I did what I had to do for my family to survive.

Before I came to St. Paul looking for food, I worked at the Hampton Inn cleaning rooms. Because I had no car, I would walk an hour and 15 minutes to work and then back home with the hot summer Florida sun beating down on me. I would arrive home dripping wet and very upset that I had to walk. I often did not have any money for lunch, and the pain of not eating was so overbearing I began to take TV dinners out of the guests' refrigerators. I also needed energy in order to work on my feet the entire time and then walk home. I was "food insecure."

WHAT IS FOOD INSECURE vs FOOD STABLE?

To me food insecure means not having money to buy needed food, or the right kind of food.

Maybe the parents are working, but only have $100 for food for the month. Many people will buy food that's not healthy because they get more quantity rather than buying quality healthy food. **Food insecure can mean scarcity but also low quality.**

People who are food insecure have to make hard choices. For example, if your child is sick, but you have no food, would you buy the medicine or the food? That's a hard choice.

I know what it's like to be food insecure. I used to eat a lot of junk and processed food because it's all I could afford. Sometimes if I had $20 to spend for food, I would buy a loaf of sliced white bread, cheese, bologna or whatever else was on sale. Then I would buy a bag of rice and beans. If I couldn't afford meat, I'd buy a dozen eggs to scramble. That's often referred to as "poor food," but it fills you.

Sometimes I would have food and sometimes I would not. (And that's why I started coming to St. Paul to get food from the pantry for my children.)

If a person is making $24,000 a year, are they able to eat healthy? Typically, the answer is "no." With a limited amount of money, many people can't afford fresh vegetables. They usually buy canned vegetables because they are cheaper. That's why we give out fresh produce at Open Arms. We don't give out canned goods, for the most part. We purposefully give them fresh food – healthy food.

Food insecure people often eat too much of the wrong things which may cause them to be overweight. Sometimes kids, who may be home alone, eat sugar-coated cereal and Twinkies, if that's what the parents buy. It fills them up when they eat a lot of cake, so they eat Twinkies and cookies.

Some people may get $200 worth of food stamps for a month. A person who has never been food insecure might judge. "They are getting food stamps, so they don't have a food insecurity problem." But $200 is nothing if you have four children in the household to feed.

Here's another example: if you were going to buy cereal, would you buy one box of Cheerios for $5 that is healthy for the children, or would you buy two boxes of generic brand frosted flakes for $5, even though it has a very large quantity of sugar in it? Food insecure individuals usually will buy the frosted flakes two for $5, because it will fill a child's stomach.

IMPROVING FOOD INSECURITY

Part of the solution for food insecurity is education. At Open Arms, we strive to provide good food, teaching them by example. This is typically what we give:

- A bag of rice
- A bag of beans
- A box of macaroni and cheese
- A can of tuna fish
- Spaghetti and spaghetti sauce
- A package of chicken and a package of ground beef
- Then they get to pick their own produce from what we have available that day.

We need to be careful of our judgmental attitudes and language toward feeding the hungry. The person sitting next to you in church might be food insecure, but you won't find that out if they hear you say something like, "Goodness, these people who come to the pantry, they are always begging." That person will not come for help because they are afraid how you will judge them. We need to be mindful of what we say when we are talking with anyone, because we don't know what's really going on in their life.

We try to develop a relationship with our clients at Open Arms, so they will reach out to us and get the help they need without feeling judged.

According to the website www.FeedingAmerica.org one out of six children in the United States may not know where they will get their next meal. That is food insecurity – they don't have enough or healthy food. Facing hunger and getting the energy they need to learn and grow is a daily challenge for more than 12 million kids in the United States.

Hunger can affect people from all walks of life. Many Americans are one job loss or medical crisis away from food insecurity. Some people, including children and seniors, may be at greater risk of hunger than others, according to that same source.

SPEAKING AT FEEDING TAMPA BAY

In 2017 I was asked to speak at a Feeding Tampa Bay Hunger Dinner. Each person who attended was randomly assigned to be **Food Secure** or **Food Insecure** and received a meal representative of that group.

Michael and Annie (a volunteer at Open Arms) attended with me and both got **Food Secure**. They ate a full meal of steak, baked potato, and vegetables, served on real dishes with napkins and actual silverware.

I got **food insecure**. I couldn't believe it!

"Food Insecure" Menu for me to choose my dinner

I was given $1.75 to "spend" for dinner. What could I buy for $1.75? These were my choices:

- Chicken $1.00 for each piece
- Green beans $.50 per ½ cup
- Slice of white bread $.25
- Water was no charge, which was good because I didn't have any money left over for juice or anything else.
- All served on a paper plate with plastic utensils.

Also on the menu were Twinkies for 10 cents each, so I could buy 17 Twinkies that would fill me up and still have some left over for the next day. (Many people will spend their limited resources on Twinkies and eat two a day to keep from feeling hungry.) That demonstrates food insecurity.

"Food Insecure" Banquet

CAN THEY REALLY CHANGE?

Many times I hear comments such as, "Why are we helping these people? There is no hope for them changing or their situation improving. We just make them dependent on us."

What they are really saying is, "I will help feed the poor so I can feel better, but I don't believe that God can actually change them or their circumstances."

However, I am living proof that God CAN and DOES change people and improve their situation. When we help others, we usually don't know what effect we have on them. We just fulfill what God asks of us and leave the results with Him. I believe that we are called to be witnesses – not judges.

I helped a young mother several years ago who came to Open Arms because she was in a domestic violence situation and was losing her children. She was mad at God. I told her my story, and told her that sometimes what is happening is a consequence for the choices we have made. God gave her the courage to be strong

36

and to believe He is with her. She disappeared, and I didn't know the outcome.

Four years later she came back and told me, "You helped me with your kind words and counsel to get my kids back. Without hearing what you shared, I would have killed myself."

We often don't know the results of what God will do in a person's life. I am blessed if He can use me and my experiences to help even one person.

I am passionate about this ministry because of what God has done for me. He not only changed my circumstances, He changed ME. My circumstances don't define who I am. I am who God says I am – wonderfully made, and with His strength I can accomplish anything.

We are all His children no matter what walk of life we come from. When we give them that bag of food, it may soften their hearts just a little. They may say, "Well, they didn't judge me today" and so they come back. Little by little they become receptive to what God can do in their lives.

We see it working in the weekly distribution at the Friday Food Fellowship at Crosspointe Church (in concert with Victor Newman Ministries, as well as Open Arms Ministry). It took us a year in God's strength with patience and diligence and obedience to really begin to see results.

People arrive early every week now and wait patiently, knowing there is going to be a devotional message before the distribution. We offer to pray privately and individually while they wait.

We see their eyes and their hearts opening. They come without any hope and leave with some hope. When you rely on your own understanding and think you don't need God in your life, you won't recognize it. But because I come from their same walk of life, I know the process for a broken person to see what God is doing and begin to trust Him.

Transformation is a process for me, and takes a long time. It just doesn't happen in one day. There were times that I would see God working, but I wouldn't pay mind to it. Or I would just quit, because God was taking too long; until I learned that it's God's timing, not my timing. When I wanted to do something in my own strength or timing, it wouldn't work out. I had to learn that it was God's will – not my will.

Our failures are part of our experiences that grow us to become who God wants us to be. If we don't fail, we won't grow. We might think we are perfect, but we aren't. We all have flaws. We may choose to deny these flaws, but God will allow us to fall to where we have no other choice but to say, "I am wrong, God. This is not the life that You want me to live, and I can't do anything without You. Without You I am nothing –zilch – not even a cent."

We see God drawing people to Himself through the process of broken people being hungry and our providing food to them. I went through it. God took me to the point where my family was hungry, and I recognized I needed Him to be in control of my life.

BEING HOMELESS

A general definition of being homeless is being without a fixed, regular, and adequate nighttime residence. It doesn't necessarily mean sleeping on the streets or a park bench or in a car.

There are two general categories of homeless: Either you are on the streets, or you are sleeping on somebody else's couch, although the legal definition to receive aid as "homeless" would disqualify people who have a support system (such as a friend providing the couch).

Becoming homeless is devastating. Going from having it all to losing everything is shattering. I don't wish that on anyone, especially when you have kids. I felt ashamed to see my children lose all their possessions: toys, clothes, everything.

I had to move to an efficiency where my two children and I lived in one room for $205 dollars a week, which was not a fixed, regular, or adequate place to live.

Since I only made $200 a week, I didn't have any money for food. I had to clean rooms at $5 a room just to be able to pay the rent and buy a few necessities.

If you don't have a way to get money, people will often take advantage of your situation with low pay for menial tasks. But I had to do what I had to do.

Then the food insecurity set in . . . not having enough money to buy my children healthy food, which means buying whatever will keep them from being hungry. I had no choice. I had to buy whatever was going to stretch.

So being homeless and hungry often go hand-in-hand.

Shame and guilt are the prevailing feelings about not having a decent place to live. I said, "Again! I have failed. I am a failure. I am worthless. I am a piece of crap for letting this happen to my children." I felt so guilty. To this day I still apologize to my daughter and my youngest son, because we had the homeless and food insecurity struggles when they were young. Sometimes I say, "I am so sorry I made you go through this."

You see, we don't realize that the mess we create means that the children get stuck with the consequences. And guess what? In reality, they struggle as adults because they remember the abuse; they remember the struggles.

So my children's hearts became hardened. The end result: when they saw someone who was struggling, they would say "Mom, you made it and helped your situation; why can't they make it?" God used me to soften their hearts, and today all four of my children volunteer at Open Arms. But it's been a process.

It took a long time for me to forgive myself for letting this happen. I knew God had forgiven me and I knew my children had forgiven me, but it's that guilt . . . how could I have let this happen? Why was I not smart enough? But of course, I was blind. I was doing everything in my own strength, without seeking the Lord's guidance.

I also didn't have anyone helping me, providing financial support or being a spiritual or emotional mentor during that time of being homeless and hungry.

CHAPTER FIVE

Helping the Outcast

While one person sees a worthless addict or homeless individual on the street sucking up the resources of the welfare system, Jesus sees a once promising intelligent person who fell on hard times and made wrong choices; a person who perhaps has lost everything and now has no one and no reason to continue on with life. Yet He sees each person as His precious child.

Ministry is what Jesus does; what He is. It isn't a business. It is real life. Jesus is walking among the outcasts; we are all outcasts, actually.

In order to really help others, I believe you have to understand their situation. Having been homeless, hungry, and without hope, I know what it feels like to be on the receiving end of programs and ministries designed to help. **Our goal at Open Arms Ministry and Victor Newman Ministries is to give a hand up, not just another hand out.**

It doesn't matter what walk of life you come from, God wants you to show His love and compassion with kindness, respecting all people. We are to give to others what God has given to us.

People who are homeless often feel like outcasts, that no one cares. I let those who come for assistance know that they are loved no matter what they have done; that we love them unconditionally, just as God unconditionally loves us. We treat them as fellow humans, with respect, because everyone deserves to be loved and respected.

We offer a kind word and encouragement. Yes, they may not listen, but when we continue to invest in them – like God invests in us – then we are developing a relationship so we can share God's Word at the appropriate time.

Before I came to St Paul looking for food, I had gone to other churches and organizations that made me feel they were doing me a favor by giving me food. I was broken and felt embarrassed and ashamed that I needed food and help. I felt judged. They looked down on me; they didn't look AT me, but DOWN on me. While they gave me the needed food, I didn't leave encouraged or hopeful, so I continued to make the same mistakes.

The world says I should be able to do life on my own, which is not true. That was pride, and that's a sin. God was working on me and wanted me to learn to humble myself and ask for help.

Usually when people come for assistance, they are really broken. They are looking for more than food. They are looking for respect and encouragement – something that will give them hope to continue moving forward and not give up.

We are not responsible for what people do, but we are responsible for sharing the Good News, for letting people know they are not alone in the path they are walking. I believe a lot of churches today are failing to do that. A large church can be so busy doing programs designed to help the less-fortunate that they don't stop to focus on the lost person standing in front of them.

Even though I still felt judged when I came to church, the difference at the pantry ministry at St. Paul was Mary Vaughn. She took me under her wing and became my mentor.

Every time I came in, Miss Mary would hug me and say, "You are loved. It doesn't matter what you have done. God has forgiven you. Learn to forgive yourself." She kept telling me the same words and quoting scriptures and saying that God was going to use me. I didn't feel judged by her.

I wouldn't look at anyone or even speak, because I was blinded by shame and bitterness, so I didn't believe her kind words initially. But Mary saw me through God's eyes. While I felt ugly, shameful, pathetic, worthless, and useless and my self-esteem was shot, slowly her words reached down into my soul and became engraved on my heart, and the Lord began to work in my life. Mary had a vision from the Lord of what I could become. Every time she sees me now, she cries. She is amazed at what God has done.

At that time, I still didn't know where I was going or what I was doing, but God was at work. Did I know anything about the pantry ministry? Not at all. All I knew is that I was lost and I needed God. It took a lot of effort and being teachable in order for me to learn what God had for me. But I had to really want it. That was all shown to me by Mary Vaughn and her love.

People who come to Open Arms or Victor Newman should not see or feel judgment. This is holy ground. They should see the love of God. If we can't show them God's love while helping them, then they will never come back, and we may lose the opportunity for Him to redeem and transform them.

God is calling us to show them they are loved and not alone, and God is with them. Yes, their current situation is a result of their attitudes and actions, but He is giving them an opportunity – again – to follow. The question is: will we – will you – choose to follow Him?

When I tell clients a little of my past story, the walls begin to come down, allowing God to work. Often they don't recognize that God will give them strength to overcome, but they need to hear what He has done for someone else, or they will continue to be lost.

Sometimes we can hear truth, but we don't believe we are worthy. A lot of people who come for assistance have made mistakes. They may be in a domestic violence situation. They want to see some kind of hope, a light. When I see the clients who come, I realize that was me not so many years ago. I am so blessed and honored that God has used me for His ministry.

I see them as children of God. It doesn't matter their situation or what they've done. They just need a little hope and faith. They need to feel loved, respected and accepted. When you have walked in those shoes as I have, you know the pain, guilt, and shame they carry.

A lot of people in the church are not accustomed to being around homeless people who haven't bathed in a week or more. So they look at them and think, "Ooh . . . I don't want him to touch me." But if God was standing there, what would He do? We have to be able to bypass our personal feelings and treat people as you would want to be treated if you were in that same situation.

DEVELOPING COMPASSION

We had one Stephen Minister volunteer who was very judgmental of the people who came for help. She would say things like, "They get food stamps; why do they come? They have jewelry or a car; why do they need food?" and so forth. I told her my story to help her understand, and she became much more compassionate towards the clients.

I am also human and can be judgmental if I'm not abiding with the Lord. When I see people come for food who are wearing nice jewelry, I remember that I had to pawn necklaces, bracelets, earrings and thousands of dollars of paintings I had bought in Greenwich Village in order to provide for my children. It is hard not to judge. I have to ask the Lord to forgive me, because we don't know what a woman had to do to get that jewelry. Many of the women who come have "sugar daddies." They settle. They settle for being with a married man to get "stuff."

God will rectify each situation as He draws them to Himself. I was involved with "dirty money," drug money. God orchestrated events so I lost everything that's dirty. God had me start over from nothing, taking away everything that was dirty. We can trust Him to work in each person's life as He sees fit. It's not my job to figure out their transformation journey but to be a catalyst for His working in their lives.

CHEATING THE SYSTEM

I am often asked about people who may be trying to "beat the system" – and what we do about it. Every story is different, but in the end, it's all the same. We are spiritually bankrupt and need God.

I learned about "cheating the system" by hearing how to do it on the streets and seeing it at other pantries. The homeless community would tell me, "Go here for this. . .; go there for that. . ." When I heard that some clients go from church to church asking for help, I asked, "Oh, my goodness; don't people get embarrassed?" I was always embarrassed and ashamed each time I had to ask for help.

I ask the clients at Open Arms, "Do you go to other pantries? This has no bearing, as we will help you whether you do or don't because this is a Christian based facility, and we aren't here to judge."

Yes, we have people who are cheating the system, who try to get food from church to church. But you know what? They really have a void in their heart. We plant a seed when we show them the love of God, while providing food. Maybe we won't see fruit now, but as we nourish that small seed, it will grow. The results are up to God.

Other places will give them food, but because that organization receives government funding, there are more restrictions on the assistance and requires much more detailed personal information, which people are often reluctant to give. We just ask for the basics so we can tell them about other appropriate programs and report back to our supporters. The Lord has directed each step, and that is how our ministry has flourished without government help.

We also ask, "How are you doing? How are you REALLY doing?" And once we establish that relationship, then we have earned the right to ask further:

"So what are you doing?"

"Why do you think you are going through this? Is it that you aren't making good choices? Because God says you have free will. You have a choice. You don't have to live this way."

See how I ask questions and make suggestions without judging them? I speak TO them – not down to them. I don't tell them what they need to do, although I try to guide them, by saying things such as:

"Why don't you try this?"

"You don't have to be afraid. God will guide you and take care of you."

"Seek God and He will give you what you really need."

"You say you want to get out of this situation, but you actually seem to be comfortable with it."

If I care more about their spiritual walk than they do, then I need to step back and let God intervene, because I am not God. I am just a vessel being used by God to help them.

At Open Arms we only provide food once a month for each client, but if they admit, "I have no food and this is my second time this month," they know I will give them what they need when they are honest. They don't have to try to cheat the system here, because we are not a "system" – we are a ministry. This is not government-run. It is God's ministry where we are called to care for the community we serve. If God brought them here, they must need something. They may not need the food, the lettuce, or the milk, but they may need spiritual food, and that is what's most important.

The elderly / shut-ins may want to talk or need someone to take them shopping because they can't easily get around. There are a lot of different ways we can help.

EXAMPLES OF IMPACT

One day I was with my friend Annie, a ministry volunteer, at a store in Pinellas Park. A woman stopped me and asked if I remembered her. (I didn't, as I see so many people.)

She said "I came to your Center. I am a veteran and had lost all of my papers, and you helped me fill out the forms so I could get my ID. Thank you so much."

And I said, "Thank the Lord, because anything I do, I do for Him. I am His vessel. I am honored that He chose me for this simple task to help you."

Recently I received a letter from a young man I had repeatedly tried to help at Open Arms. Steve (not his real name) was in and out of trouble and rehab until being sentenced to an inpatient program where he celebrated his 20th birthday. He began to learn coping skills and achieved his goal of earning his high school diploma. This is an excerpt from his letter to me:

I want to thank you for always having faith in me and never losing hope. It honestly really means a lot – everything that you did for my mother and me during our rough times. Thank you again for having faith in me. I love you, my second mom!

And that's my reward – that God would use me to do His work. I don't do things to get a pat on the back. I don't like the limelight. I don't even like speaking in front of crowds. I just like to do what God tells me to do and keep it simple.

I see clients' demeanor when they arrive at Open Arms, and I see how they laugh and smile when they leave. Our mission is to give people hope and faith so when they leave they know God is with them, a God who loves them.

WHAT I LOOK FOR IN A VOLUNTEER

The love of God in your heart and your motivation are the two main qualities I value in a volunteer. Why do you want to volunteer? Do you want to be seen, or do you do it because this is your passion, your gift? Do you do it because you love the Lord? Are you committed? Or are you obligated?

Many people want to be part of the ministry because of our size and results, but to be in outreach ministry, you have to have the heart and passion for it from the Lord.

Most people who come here are broken – clients AND volunteers. The ones who think they aren't broken, they actually are, which is evidenced by their judgmental attitude. Sometimes God will bring them here for a season to learn. I can learn organization and process from them, and they can learn from me what not to do in relating to clients.

I tell them, "We deal with broken people, and you must understand we all have issues and are all God's children. We have to be able to minister to them and let them know they are not alone. If you cannot do that, you are in the wrong ministry. I won't allow anyone to be treated with disrespect or feel worthless or shameful."

For those who can't lovingly accept and understand our clients, we refer them to another ministry in the church for which they may be better suited.

I have found that many people want to "help the poor" because of the good feeling it gives them. They are concerned about their own conscience, not necessarily whether their "help" actually meets the need.

True compassion means seeing the person as a child of God and giving them what they really need – hope and encouragement – not just money or what they ask for.

I attempt to demonstrate and model how I want the volunteers to interact with the clients. If I'm talking it, I'm walking it. If a client starts cursing, and I curse back, they will see me as a hypocrite. I have to be able to back up talk with actions.

I also keep it simple. As time goes by, volunteers' hearts soften and their eyes open, because they see that we truly care for the clients. We have standard procedures that God has helped me establish, and I am firm in explaining – with love – that they must be followed. So if the volunteers are teachable and can follow procedures, they can learn to show God's love, respect and compassion.

St. Paul didn't put me at Open Arms. God did. Everything that has happened, God has done. I wasn't capable of doing this on my own.

Today I am able to empathize with clients and volunteers, so they know that I understand how they feel because I was also an outcast and am now allowing God to use me as His volunteer!.

CHAPTER SIX

The Growth and Ministry of Open Arms

When I first came as a client and then as a volunteer to Open Arms, it was just one small room, and no one worked in it very much. Mary Vaughn handed out food, while Shaun Powers gave general staff oversight. After about a year I was given a key and responsibility for the panty, because I was there every day. The only other volunteer at that time was Nancy Missette, who has witnessed my growth, along with the growth of the ministry.

In the beginning we were helping about 30 people a week; then we began to expand: 20 people a day; then 500 a month. We outgrew the small pantry room and moved across the street.

At first people who needed help didn't like coming to Open Arms, because St. Paul was such a large and prestigious church that they were afraid they would be judged. But in time, as our actions reflected the love of the Lord, doors opened, not only to the community but also to business partnerships.

When a person walks in, I don't want them to see my face; I want them to see Jesus, the love of God. That is my passion.

I volunteered six years before I was hired as staff when Pastor Bob Martin came to St. Paul. I didn't ask to be the Director. I certainly didn't ask to be the Coordinator. Everything just happened according to God's plan, so my official title today is "Director of Open Arms Ministry."

RECORD KEEPING

Since the church hadn't been keeping pantry records, in 2010 I began to write down basic information on a sheet of notebook paper. For the first six months of 2010, we gave out 425 bags of food. We distributed homeless bags, pizza, chicken and bread. No produce in the beginning.

[**A homeless bag** is different than the regular bags we distribute, because people living in the streets cannot cook and may not have a can opener. A homeless bag consists of fruit, a drink, maybe a sandwich, a bag of chips, things that they don't have to cook. They are able just to open it and eat it.]

The church was amazed at the number of people we were helping and how much food we handed out. (That's why keeping records is important!) From August to October of 2010, we fed 1,113 families. We were only getting small gift card donations for $20 to $50 to help buy food; very little.

In 2013 I realized we needed a better method for keeping records than by hand, not only to keep them confidential, but also so they could not get lost or destroyed. When I spoke at a 211 Tampa Bay conference, God guided me to discover an on-line software system: www.pantryworx.com. In February 2014, we began to enter thousands of files into this computerized tracking system.

The basic information we collect helps us to know the individuals and geographic areas we are serving, and allows us to accurately report to our supporters. It also enables us to stop those who try to beat the system, even though we help everyone who comes.

Today we average 3,200 people a month who visit Open Arms. Each person represents a household. So we are actually feeding over 7,000 people each month.

We also give food to other churches to distribute to their communities. God is calling us to step out of the church and reach out to others – not just those in our circle.

FINANCIAL / BUDGET FOR OPEN ARMS

St. Paul United Methodist Church takes care of the building and utilities, and the United Methodist Women raise other support. Business partners and individuals donate clothing, food and money.

In 2012 we started giving limited, temporary financial assistance to those who are on the verge of having their electricity shut off. The "Love Fund," comes from donations by our church members and one of our ministry business partners. We pay $50 towards each bill for five people a month. It takes a lot of discernment to ascertain which people should receive the assistance. People may have the money to pay their electricity, but hold off doing so, thinking that the church will pay it. Our policy is that if we have helped them three times over their lifetime, that's our limit, since this is not a long-term solution. We help with food and clothes, and we recommend other organizations (resources) to those needing more long term assistance.

BACK TO SCHOOL OUTREACH

In August we do a Back-to-School event where we help 500-600 children with school uniforms and book bags / back packs filled with school supplies.

We buy the backpacks from 211 Tampa Bay for $7 each, paid for by the United Methodist Women – about $3,000.

Here is one example of how good God is. In October 2016 I received a call, "Yvette, come and pick up supplies for the school outreach for next year." So we had supplies for backpacks a year in advance!

Each year we also collect new school uniforms that will be handed out before back-to-school, as uniforms are often a financial burden for many families.

THANKSGIVING OUTREACH

The Monday before Thanksgiving we have a special food distribution to provide a Thanksgiving Dinner to about 400 families. While much of the food is donated, we actually buy turkeys.

Let me tell you what God did several years ago! Pastor Pam reported, "Everywhere I go, they are charging $1.99 a pound for turkeys." We agreed that was too expensive, as we could not spend almost $5,000 for turkeys.

I told her, "God has a plan."

A few days later Walmart called, "Yvette, you were asking about turkeys? We are going to give you 400 turkeys at $.59 a pound!" Now who does that? That was God alone. You can't lose when you are on His team. You have to wait and see what He is going to do when you trust Him.

CHRISTMAS OUTREACH

We take applications to help 500+ children at Christmas, as the Lord provides resources. We also give a bag of food to the family for a holiday dinner that includes either a ham or turkey.

We used to hand out bags of pre-selected toys, but we changed our process, because I remember how embarrassed I felt when I didn't have enough money to buy toys for my kids, and I got presents from the church. My kids always knew where they came from, so they realized the presents weren't really from me.

Our revised process is intended to give parents dignity. About a week and a half before Christmas, we set up the gym at St. Paul UMC where people go to "shop" for toys to give their children, which they don't pay for. They choose toys from a wide selection, and wrap them with paper we provide. Then THEY give the presents to their children.

I have learned and experienced that when we do things the way God wants them done, He provides. We get donations from our business partners and from church members, who are generous. One person last year gave $5,000, because she knows what we do. We have worked hard to guard our integrity, to be sure that our actions match our words, and we are truly helping the community we serve.

PARTNERSHIPS WITH BUSINESSES

We currently accept donations from more than seven different companies or organizations that help provide the food we distribute to the community. God put everything in place. I didn't go looking for these partnerships; they found me. They came asking what we need. God is the one who is arranging all this. It's not a people movement, but a God movement.

Our partnerships with local businesses and organizations have developed over time. They have watched our consistency, our integrity and whether we really believe and do what we are professing. People can say and promise anything, but do we believe in our ministry and follow through. Our integrity is critical to healthy on-going partnerships.

The business relationships started when a woman from a large retailer called out of nowhere, asking to partner with us. Usually, this company requires a rigorous application process, but God orchestrated it that they came to me. She said they heard what we were doing, and asked me to speak at a company meeting.

You know how sometimes you plan what you are going to say, but then God changes it? That's what happened! I told them my passion is serving the Lord and the community because I was one of them. I am one of them. I am an outcast. When they heard my story, it's like the floodgates of heaven opened, and everything started pouring down. I said, "This is from God! He did this. Thank you, Lord!"

Then it went on to another vendor, and another and another. Now it's expanded to where we are able to help other churches. I make sure that these churches are not only giving food, but also spreading the Good News of Jesus.

BIGGEST NEED AT OPEN ARMS

Not everyone needs money, but this is the way our world thinks. They believe that more money will fix all their problems, but that's not true.

Think about it this way: a child wants his dad to spend more time with him, but the father just hands him $5. Buying something isn't what the child really needs.

Today society has it so messed up. We want to give everybody things, but we fail to give them what is most important: our heart, our time, our presence. People want to know that you are present with them and listening to them. It's not all about money, nor is it just about a bag of food. People often come just to talk or request prayer.

Although we can always use more money, that's not our biggest need. We need more people, people who are passionate about the Lord and following Him. We need spiritual mentors, people who are willing to come alongside others and show the love of God, to disciple and invest in their lives, to show them a better way. They need to know that they are not alone and that God loves them.

CONNECTING CLIENTS TO THE CHURCH

I invite clients to church all the time. Recently four people came to Crosspointe Church for Friday Food Fellowship (food distribution). They are very broken. When I saw them, I loved on them and told them not to give up, that God hasn't given up on them, and their cries do not go unnoticed by Him.

Whenever I talk with anyone looking for help, I vividly remember my shame in asking for food, and how I thought nobody cared.

They said "We just love the church because you show so much love." I responded, "What you see is the love of God that He has for you. It isn't me. It's Him. He is using me to let you know that He loves you. Why don't you come to church on Sunday? I'll be there and if you feel uncomfortable, you can sit with me. God wants you to be His guest, and you will be amazed at what He wants to do in your life. You will never be the same again."

While I talk about the church and invite them, I don't guilt or make it a condition for them to get food. We don't want them to feel obligated. If people feel obligated to come in return for what we gave them, they often will resent the church.

We want them to be drawn to the church. They get drawn in by sensing God's love through us and becoming committed. I want them to commit to the Lord – not commit to the pastor or to me. Once they are in the door of the church, they will feel the love of God, if the people greet them warmly and are open and not phony and treat them with respect and dignity.

VOLUNTEERS

Most of the 75 volunteers at Open Arms attend St. Paul UMC. We also do a homeless feeding twice a month in downtown Clearwater in conjunction with Victor Newman Ministries. There are about 125 total volunteers for the "Community Catering" (homeless feeding), together with both ministries.

We also host a food distribution ministry at Crosspointe Community Church, Lake Palms Campus on Fridays with Victor Newman Ministries. In 2018 we distributed food to over 15,000 people. God has orchestrated a team of volunteers who faithfully help every week, many from the community.

Since Michael and I live in the community, some of the people who come FOR help are getting involved. When they see what we are doing and that God is shining His light on the ministry, they are drawn to help.

That's how Annie got involved. Annie lives near the church. One day she came to the Friday Food Fellowship just to see what was going on. First she started volunteering, and then she began coming to church and was baptized. After that she was spiritually mentored. Her faith and relationship with the Lord have grown significantly. Simply showing the love of God opened the doors of her heart. Now she works closely with me daily at Open Arms and Victor Newman Ministries.

Yvette with Anne Schaffner

That's our purpose and goal: that the love of God will open the eyes and hearts of the people of the community who are living apart from God, and that they seek Him.

THE NEXT CAMPUS

In the summer of 2018, the Lord provided a new location to house the Open Arms Ministry in a former church property three miles from our original location. Known as St. Paul UMC, Druid Campus, it is on a bus route and easily accessible for the clients God has chosen for us to serve.

The campus is larger, which will allow us to expand ministry and services. As God leads, future plans may include a small church, Bible Study and discipleship classes, and other community classes and events, since there are classrooms and storage, as well as a sanctuary.

God is continuing to grow Open Arms Ministry to impact the community for the Lord.

CHAPTER SEVEN

[Almost] Final Thoughts

1 John 1:8-9 says *If we claim to be without sin, we deceive ourselves and the truth is not in us. But if we confess our sins, He is faithful and just and will forgive us our sins and purify us from all unrighteousness.* (NIV)

If we ask for forgiveness, God gives us the opportunity to get things right. And this is what God has done in my life.

I was very naïve. When I began coming to church, I expected Christians to be "perfect" and not gossip or judge. I have learned from these 1 John verses that we all sin. You see, sin is being disobedient to God, plain and simple. We are all broken and fall short whether we go to church, help in a ministry or live on the street.

What doesn't change is God. He loves us all and gives us all the same opportunity to come to Him so He can transform us into the image of His Son.

With this book I pray your eyes and heart will be opened to what God is saying to you. No matter what path you are currently on, God loves each of us as His children, and is calling you and me into an intimate relationship with Him.

What God did for me, He can do for anyone. That is why I wrote my story. We all need to be vulnerable, so God's light can shine through our experiences and draw others to Him.

What led me to use my experiences to help others? The Lord did. It took me all these years to understand that God was always with me. He gave me the opportunities, but I initially refused to see them. When I let Him, He began to unravel my crazy life and gave me the life He always wanted for me, the unique one He created me for. All that I have gone through, however, has given me the compassion, passion, and ability to minister to others.

I compare God's healing to a fruit tree. In my own strength, I kept cutting off diseased branches. I decided to just cut "this" off; or chop "that" off. But the problem was at the root. All the abuse, the rape, the abandonment, the domestic violence was all still down there in my roots. I was just cleaning up my outward appearance, and ignored the underlying root cause of my poor decisions. So I had to let God work on the roots of my heart, and heal the deep hurts from my past.

Although there were consequences for my choices, the pain that I experienced was converted to a gain. While I didn't recognize it when I was in the middle of it, I would never have walked into St. Paul and found God had I not needed food.

I think people often believe that there is no hope for the "outcasts" to change. But I am a living example of the grace and mercy of God and what HE can do! He CAN change people and their circumstances!

I am still a work in progress. God is not finished with me. I get up every morning and ask, "Lord, what do you want me to do today? Please guide me." It doesn't matter – whatever He says I will do.

Today, God is faithfully pruning me. . .which can make me uneasy when I sense Him approaching. But He speaks calmly into my heart, "I'm going to prune only those things that keep you from producing more spiritual fruit." Pruning is necessary, as Jesus says in John 15:2. Consequently, the gardener carefully prunes so we can produce more abundant fruit. Why? Fruit feeds others. It sustains and nourishes. We have the confidence that God will make us spiritually fruitful, if we submit ourselves to pruning and allow Him to live and abide in us.

My son recently asked, "If God knows we are doing something wrong, why doesn't He stop us?" I answered that it's because God has given us free will. Could you imagine if God forced everyone to love Him? Then we would be like robots. God doesn't want that. He wants you to choose to love Him and let Him direct your life. He gives you the opportunity to do what's right. If you choose to do the wrong thing, it's not because He doesn't love you. He loves you that much to let you do what you want and discover that you are incomplete without Him.

God didn't let me make those choices because He didn't love me. I made mistake after mistake and got so lost I didn't know where to turn. After I found myself on the floor in that garage on my face, I cried out to God to save me. Sometimes we fall so far down that we don't have any choice but to look up.

If I had known then what I know now, I wouldn't have made those mistakes. But if I hadn't made those mistakes, I wouldn't be where I am today. So either way, God is using what I have gone through for His glory.

Yes, sometimes I doubt, but God has me 100%. I can't let go of God or I will be broken again. He has brought me to where I am, and has given me a passion and a ministry.

Today I prefer to have what money can't buy. What money buys can be lost or taken away at any time, but what God has given me, no one can take away. It's priceless.

If I could choose to go through everything again to get to where I am, I would do so. It's been a painful journey. But look at Jesus. He was sinless and was mocked, abused, persecuted, and killed. I knew He was going to help me get through this painful time of healing.

These last years have been an unbelievable journey of ongoing personal development in my spiritual walk. Once I came to the understanding of God as Creator, and who I am as His Creation, then I began living in the realm God designed for me. God is the critical connection that puts my life into rhythm, balance, and alignment with Him and others.

For those who are homeless and hungry, my prayer is that my story may encourage you to cry out to God, who is the solution for your struggles.

If you have been impacted by my story, I pray you will feel compelled to invest in the lives of others, giving words of encouragement and hope and not judgment and condemnation, showing Jesus to all who need Him.

[NOTE: Yvette thought this was the final chapter, the end of the book, but God was bringing challenging experiences into her life, as she shares in the Epilogue.]

CHAPTER EIGHT

Epilogue:
October / November 2018

When you think that life is all settled and you are doing everything right, life throws you a curve ball when you least expect it, and that's what happened to me.

I had not been feeling well since March 2018 and inexplicably began losing a lot of weight. Michael needed to finish some ordination classes by April. I knew that if I told him I was ill, he would stop working on his courses, so I kept quiet about the pain I was experiencing.

Seeing Michael ordained by the Free Methodist Church in April 2018 was one of the happiest days of my life, because I had waited and waited and prayed on it. I saw a vision five or six years ago that he would be ordained, so I knew what God was going to do in his life, and I didn't want to be the cause of his not reaching that goal.

Michael's ordination, April 20, 2018

Like I said, life was going along normally, and then everything went "bam." I thought I had a large hemorrhoid. During a routine colonoscopy in July, the doctor found it was a mass in my colon. The next six weeks of tests resulted in a diagnosis of Stage 4 colon cancer. I had a growth in my groin, as well as a larger mass in my colon.

I cried when I first heard the diagnosis. I didn't know how to tell Michael. The only person I could turn to was the Lord.

The emotional pain was as hard as the physical pain. I realized I was fighting a battle with the devil. You see, the closer I get to the Lord, the more intense the struggle.

I began an aggressive treatment of chemotherapy and radiation in September in an attempt to shrink the cancer, so the growths could be removed by surgery, unless the treatment eliminated them altogether.

In mid-September I was rushed to the hospital with excruciating pain. I cried; Michael cried; my daughter cried. You can't imagine how bad the pain was.

I said, "Lord, I don't know if I can do this. I know I can't do it without You. I don't think You have brought me this far for all this to happen, but I accept it." I have to accept it to be at peace.

I am at peace – in the midst of the pain. It's not easy. I want to say "Why, God?" But I don't. I am not mad at God.

Through it all, I go to the Lord. I don't talk to people, because they have different perspectives, and although they try to help, sometimes they say thoughtless and mean things, and they don't realize it. They don't think before they speak. Someone came up to me and said, "You look so terrible." That worked negatively on me for a whole week. The last thing I need is for someone to give me an inferiority complex or lots of advice.

It's not only dealing with the cancer, it is also handling my emotions. I was going through a little depression because when I look in the mirror, I see how much weight I have lost. I look like a little girl; I don't have any breasts and I am losing my hair. The enemy tries to attack me by telling me that my husband is not going to look at me as a woman. On the other hand, I also have to watch my weight because sugar feeds the cancer.

I talk a lot to the Lord in the middle of the night. I often get up in excruciating pain to sit on the couch since I can hardly sleep, trying to let Michael rest. That's when I cry out, "Lord, please, help me make it through the next hour. Please show me what to do and help me with the pain. I need to feel your presence; I need it right now." And the Holy Spirit showers me with grace, and then I'm okay again.

MY MOTHER

Another blow came when my mother was admitted to the hospital on September 20 with cancer in her lymph nodes that had spread to her spleen and liver. We had no idea she had it. On a Sunday in early September, she had come to bring me soup. That day she told me, "I don't want to have to bury you. I am not going to do that."

**Yvette and Mother Carmen in June, 2018,
before knowing we both had cancer**

My doctor finally cleared me to visit my mom in the hospital, because it was driving her crazy that she couldn't see me. I had to wear a mask to prevent any additional bacteria from entering my body.

She kissed my hand and told me, "I asked the Lord that if He is going to take one of us that He take me, because I have lived my life and your work is not done."

I know that the Lord doesn't bargain. When it's your day, it's your day, but that is what she had been praying. That just broke me. And I thought, "Why is she saying this to me? Lord, I can't make sense of all this. I just can't."

My family had to decide whether to do chemotherapy on my mother. Knowing how much it had knocked me down (and I am 20 years younger than Mom), my sister decided not to put her through all the additional pain of the chemo. The doctors and nurses worked to control her pain and to make her last days as comfortable as possible.

On October 5 I received a call that I needed to come immediately to see my mother, so Peter came to take me. I had just finished a radiation treatment, but I didn't get there in time.

God called my Mom home to be with Him that day at age 83. The last time I saw her was the Friday before she died. I wasn't expecting her to be that sick and go so fast. I am shocked. I am at a loss for words. That's been an additional challenge, making me even more dependent on the Lord.

After the funeral when I came home, I realized I hadn't grieved properly. I hadn't cried because my diagnosis and pain and my mom's death were all mixed up. So much for me to handle, but God is helping me a day at a time.

TREATMENT

One day at my radiation treatment, all the nurses seemed to have an attitude, and Claryvette got irritated. I told her that you have to be humble, because you don't know what others are going through. People come here by themselves and are upset because they don't have anyone with them. The hurting patients take it out on the nurses, making their job very hard, but one smile, one "how are you doing?" can change their perspective.

Then I told her "watch this." A nurse came in and I asked, "How is your day today?" She smiled and replied that most people don't ask her that. I said, "Well, you matter, too. God uses you to help us."

Within minutes Claryvette could see the entire atmosphere in the room change. The nurses, the patients, everyone seemed more peaceful. I said, "See? I may be the only Bible that she 'reads', so I can't be mad at her." The patients in treatment can be nasty because of the pain. It's overwhelming. It wears on everyone. So I try to be cordial and polite, and I speak to them about the Lord a lot.

One nurse asked me how I was doing, and I replied, "Day by day, hanging onto the Lord." She said people don't talk about the Lord there. Thus, it's a very distressing and depressing place. While the employees can't speak about God, they can't stop me from doing so. That's what I do to keep focused and my mind off of my own situation.

Before this all happened, my family was bickering over many things, but now they are united, which brings me great joy and peace. When I need to rest, I rest in God and constantly speak with Him.

When I'm in pain, I scream out to the Lord. And Michael cries. He is beside himself. It is so hard on him to see me in pain, because he can't do anything about it. He wants to fix it but he can't. I tell him, "I'm sorry you have to go through this. I know you didn't sign up for this." He tells me I don't have to apologize, but I know the agony he is going through. He tells me he needs me and to please fight. And I am fighting. He doesn't want me to give up.

I pray for Michael, because something this hard could cause anyone to fall back. He used to use drugs, and anything this difficult can trigger a relapse. He is strong in the Lord, however, and I have a lot of faith in him. I pray for him and tell him to go to the food distribution or the homeless feeding for Victor Newman.

The enemy attacks me on any little thing, especially about Michael. I start to think if anything happens to me, maybe he will get remarried within a year. Who knows? When I am in heaven I won't care, but the enemy knows it will hurt my heart while I am here.

While Michael is the man God chose for me and he is a wonderful encourager, I know that he is not my god. I adore my husband. I watch Michael to make sure this isn't overwhelming him. He will suffer if anything else should happen to me. I told him, "God has a plan for you, too. We don't know if He is going to give us our own church to shepherd or what His plans are."

Both my son and my husband gave the doctors a hard time when I was in so much pain because I got an overdose of chemotherapy drugs. I have never seen Michael so upset, because he felt it was a preventable thing.

Michael told me I was way too forgiving. I responded, "Michael, they aren't God. They are used by God but they also fall short, so we have to pray for them." (Meanwhile I am in excruciating pain!)

Then I hugged the doctor and told him, "Thank you for all you are doing. I know it's not your fault because you aren't God."

He just looked at me. Then I said, "You are being used by God, but you aren't God. I seek and trust God. I have to go through you, seeking Him. Every time I see that doctor now, he says, "God bless you." You bring the Holy Spirit with you everywhere you go.

I hug my doctors and tell them that I pray for them every day, because their jobs are not easy. They are a tool God is using to heal me; but my faith is in the Lord.

Yvette and Peter, on way to radiation treatment, October, 2018

My children have a schedule to take me to treatments, while Michael continues to do the ministry. It's also been good that other people have stepped up to help with many of the tasks we have always done. That is also part of God's plan.

God has prepared Annie to take on more responsibility at Open Arms, since she retired this year, and I have been ill. I am empowering her, because that's what we are supposed to do. The Apostle Paul says in Ephesians 4:12 that we are to equip / empower people to do ministry; that's leadership. Others have also stepped up, so Open Arms and Victor Newman will continue, as God provides.

Every day for six weeks, I have been getting chemotherapy and then I go to radiation. The most pain recently is the burning from the radiation. I just finished my last treatment on October 24, so now I heal and wait.

It's not easy. Some days are good and others not so good. But God has given me the strength. Did I expect all this? No.

I have always had compassion for people who are sick, but now I have a whole new perspective! My relationship with the Lord has gotten stronger through all this, as well.

I don't question God. I really don't. At first, I asked, "What did I do wrong?" And then I recognized that the devil is a liar. I said, "Lord, I know you have me. I just don't understand." At the end I will understand, no matter what happens. When I get to heaven, I won't care. But it's scary. I'm frightened for my husband. I love my husband, or we wouldn't have made it this far.

When I was diagnosed with cancer and was in so much pain, I read a lot from the book of Job, and I would put myself in his story. It's like the devil said, "What can I do to Yvette and Michael that will sidetrack them or get them to curse the Lord?"

Me? I have cancer; I've lost weight; I've lost my Mom. I go through self-doubt, but I haven't cursed the Lord. I haven't questioned Him. I just say, "Lord, please help me today." But God is faithful. God has me, and slowly I am healing and am at peace.

I don't know how I would have survived this without my faith in God, especially during the treatments and pain. I prayed non-stop. I still do. I couldn't move without pain; going to the bathroom, taking a shower, sitting down. I don't know how people who don't have the Lord survive something like this.

The pain and this experience have also strengthened the bond between Michael and me. We realize how precious someone is when we might lose them. I've learned so much since April, because God is teaching me.

I also look at people differently and now give them more grace, because I just don't know what they are going through. Are they in my path because they are seeking the Lord? I don't know what is happening in their homes nor what God is doing in their lives. So I need to forgive, because I also have fallen short. I can't judge others. I know that if I judge someone, I better be sure I am not living in that glass house myself!

What's important to me is the Lord, Michael, my children and grandchildren, my family, and my church family.

God is also bringing my children along. I hear them speaking more about God now and going to church more often. They are beginning to understand what I have been telling them about the Lord is true and it's important.

I have also learned to empathize with people who have cancer because when I was whining, I thought about the babies who are not even able to communicate that they are in pain. I reflect on the elders who get mistreated because they are in so much pain and don't have a family member to advocate for them.

I am scared. It doesn't mean I don't have faith. I am human. If I have to have surgery, I may have to wear a bag, which would change my perspective of myself as a woman. It's a lot to handle, but with the Lord I know that I am going to make it.

I hope sharing my experiences will help others not to give up. I don't know what the future holds for me. I just know I am in God's hands, and I trust Him.

Am I afraid of leaving my husband? Absolutely. And my children? Yes. My family? Sure, but I have to trust them to God.

I know that no matter what happens, I will be victorious. Either He will enable me to train and involve more people to carry on the ministry and I will be with Him in heaven, or He wants me to continue doing His work here on earth. Either way I am victorious.

PROGRESS

Praise the Lord, because we just found out that the growth in my groin lymph node is gone! And the other large tumor in my colon is shrinking. Next we wait to do a PET scan in December to see exactly what's going on and pray the doctor can do surgery which will have its own challenges. Some of my energy is returning. I won't gain all my weight back fully, but I will gain some of it back. I will see what else God has for me to do.

So that's where I am at this point in my life.

And God keeps telling me it's important to finish this book and tell my story.

If people get anything from reading my story, it is that you should never give up, or lose hope. Also, seek the Lord and trust Him. Everything comes from Him. If we don't have that relationship with Him, we are lost.

My story is important, I believe, for those who have cancer, those who have been homeless and hungry – and those who are trying to help minister to people in those circumstances.

Glory to God!

[NOTE: for an update on Yvette, visit the Victor Newman website. www.VictorNewman.org]

Yvette and Michael in Victor Newman Ministry shirts, October, 2018

Box truck donated by Baycare to Victor Newman Ministries

Michael preaching in September 2018

Family – Michael took the picture!
Front row: daughter Claryvette, sister Marissa, niece Alyssa,
niece Ariana, niece Isis, Michael's mother Barbara;
Back row: Jose, son Miguel, son Peter, brother Ozzie, mother Carmen,
son Robert, and Yvette

With Michael's children Marcus and Ebony

Daughter Claryvette and grandchildren Jeremiah, Miah and Gabriel

Yvette and Michael

Yvette with son Peter and his children: Sarah, Xylena, Gabriel, Bethany, Sophia

Son Miguel (Miggie) with his son Matthew, "my baby's baby"

Yvette

CHAPTER NINE

30 Devotionals for Prayer and Meditation

A PENNY FOR YOUR THOUGHTS

I wrote these devotionals for you to grow in your relationship with the Lord – whether you need hope and help or are being obedient to the Lord in offering hope and help to others.

Please don't just read them all at one sitting.

I encourage you to read one devotional each day, meditating on the Scripture, and asking God what He has for you to understand. Then obey what you hear Him saying! Take action!

Blessings, Yvette

DAY 1 – Unconditional Love

JOHN 15:12 *This is my commandment: Love each other in the same way I have loved you.* NLT

Never waste the opportunity to express God's love to others.

Love is a choice. It's a commitment. Do you ever wonder why we constantly seek love from others but never feel completely satisfied? God designed us for unconditional love that only He can give. Because all people are flawed, however, we often continue to seek that love from others but will not find it there.

God wants you to find your need for love and acceptance fulfilled in Him. Only after experiencing and knowing the unconditional love that God has for you, the love that drove God to send his Son to earth to die for you, can you begin to love others with the same quality of unconditional love.

Unconditional love has nothing to do with romance. It does not want anything FROM the other person, though it may want everything FOR them. It is not about desire and possession; it is about appreciation and concern. Don't let the opinions of others make you forget that.

When the Holy Spirit urges you to show unconditional love to someone else, do it. Reach out in a sensitive, caring way, not talking down to a person. As a disciple of Jesus Christ, share Christ's Love and His Word with those who are hurting There is no exercise better for the heart than reaching out and lifting people up.

Have a blessed day and may the unconditional love of the Lord be with you.

DAY 2 – How Does God See Me?

EPHESIANS 1:4 *For he chose us in him before the creation of the world to be holy and blameless in his sight.* NIV

How do you see yourself? Have you ever wondered how God sees you? I used to. Then one day I asked Him, and He answered through His Word.

As He took me through Scripture, I was amazed at God's perception of me and realized that He doesn't see me as I see myself.

While at times we perceive ourselves as failures, God doesn't. So many of us base our self-worth on how others see us or on our accomplishments or lack of achievements. Perhaps we feel shame from our past and define our value based on our looks or on others' opinions.

God sees how some people have helped you, and others have hurt you. He sees your disappointments, your fears, your failures and how all these things have changed you in good and bad ways. He also sees your desire to be greater than your past.

He chose you! If you look at yourself and others like God does, you will realize you are important and you will come to greater knowledge of Him than you have ever experienced.

Ask God how He sees you. You'll never reach the potential that He has for you while trying to do "the best you can" through your own efforts. He knows you can do better with His guidance and help.

You see, God is never wrong. You may not feel worthy, but God says you ARE worthy – worthy to receive ALL that He has and wants for you. It's about your faith, not your feelings.

I encourage you, from this time forward – no looking back – begin seeing yourself through the eyes of God and be blessed!

DAY 3 – Forgiveness

LUKE 23:34 *Father, forgive them, for they do not know what they are doing.* NIV

Forgiveness as described in the Bible is one of the greatest blessings that God has given us, and one of the greatest blessings we can give to others.

Often forgiveness isn't easy. Betrayal and abuse can hurt (both emotionally and physically), which can cause us to struggle with true forgiveness. In fact, we can sometimes hurt ourselves worse by not forgiving the people in our lives, as opposed to simply forgiving them and moving on.

Family drama can be very frustrating and difficult. The first family in the Bible was dysfunctional. Cain killed his brother Abel. That's very dramatic. And afterward, Cain had to leave his home, as God commanded.

The same is true with many Bible "greats." Abraham left his family to follow God's will. Jesus said that sometimes mother and daughter, father and son, will be divided because of His sake.

Sometimes we must separate ourselves from family members and others who continue to cause us pain, or who do not follow God. However, we must be sure to forgive them and always love them with God's help.

We also need to create new boundaries when people have harmed us. It is very hard to forgive people who never admit wrong, who never apologize, and who never change their ways.

Today I encourage you to forgive anyway and let go of the pain. Give it to God. He will help you.

Have a blessed day and may the forgiveness of the Lord be with you.

DAY 4 – The Next Right Step

PSALM 37:4 *Take delight in the Lord, and he will give you your heart's desires.* NLT

Until faith comes to our hearts, we cannot expect an illumination of the Word of God that gives us understanding of the purposes of God.

It has been said that the peace of God rests where the peace of God reigns.

I don't know what you are dealing with in your life. I only know that our God is bigger. It may seem like your situation is impossible and that you have no way out, but God is not limited by any restrictions or boundaries. He sees the beginning and end of your life, and all things have been worked out, even if you can't see it yet. God has given you the strength, so get up and "pick up your mat and walk," just as Jesus told the man he healed in John 5:8.

All spiritual journeys are unique, but they have common steps along the way. The steps are not set in order for everyone, and don't always occur in a particular way. God will guide you along your unique journey.

At times you may get off track. That's common. But when you do get off track, ask God to show you the next right step. God knows what is in your heart. Be open to Him and willing to listen and obey Him.

God won't kick down the door of your heart. He will knock gently and wait for you to open the door, as described in Revelation 3:20.

Have a blessed day and may the peace of the Lord be with you as you take delight in the Lord and open the door of your heart to Him – and take the next right step.

DAY 5 – Choices; God is the Answer

PROVERBS 23:7 *For as he thinks in his heart, so is he. "Eat and drink!" he says to you, But his heart is not with you.* NKJV

Often people tell me that they want to change their ways, but don't do anything to accomplish that change. What about you? Do you want to change your ways? Do you REALLY want your circumstances to be different? Lack of motivation is a major reason people do not change. However, when we are determined that serving God is our most important purpose in life, then we will find the means to allow Him to make the necessary changes.

Sometimes we get overwhelmed, and negative thinking takes over. We get distracted. We all have days when nothing seems to go right; everything breaks; pieces don't fit; everything we touch spills. I have seen many people convince themselves that change is impossible for them, that it's too late. They often blame their circumstances for who they have become. You see, to a certain degree we control our own destiny because God has given us free will. We control our own lives with the choices we make. Someone might say "You just don't understand my circumstance. You just don't know what kind of a father I have, or what kind of a mother I have, or what has happened to me."

But God is telling us that enough is enough. He wants to change the way we think. Before we can change our ways, we must allow God to change our mind. I believe in the principle that you ought to act "as if" you were the person you would like to become. As you do that, you will grow into that kind of person, as you allow God to transform you on the inside. Ultimately, your actions and your attitude that God is placing in you will lead you into being the person that God created you to be.

God sees that you are searching for answers, but don't know where to look. God is the answer. As you trust God, He will change your attitudes and actions because He is in the business of changing lives!

Today I challenge you: turn everything over to the Lord. It's time to stop complaining, arguing and speaking negatively and start following God and doing what's right. It's your choice.

Have a blessed day as you choose God. Get on His course, and be confident of who GOD has made you to be and His plans for your life

DAY 6 – Homeless

MATTHEW 25:34-40 [Jesus said] *Then the King will say to those on his right, "Come, you who are blessed by my Father; take your inheritance, the kingdom prepared for you since the creation of the world. For I was hungry, and you fed me. I was thirsty, and you gave me a drink. I was a stranger, and you invited me into your home. I was naked, and you gave me clothing. I was sick, and you cared for me. I was in prison, and you visited me."*

Then these righteous ones will reply, "Lord, when did we ever see you hungry and feed you? Or thirsty and give you something to drink? Or a stranger and show you hospitality? Or naked and give you clothing? When did we ever see you sick or in prison and visit you?"

And the King will say, "I tell you the truth, when you did it to one of the least of these my brothers and sisters, you were doing it to me!" NIV

Have you ever wondered what to say or do when you see a homeless person?

Most of us tend to have the same response: We avoid eye contact and walk a little faster. But you might also wonder about their situation, thinking, "What's his story? How did this happen to her? How long have they lived on the streets?" Maybe you even wanted to help but didn't know how to start a conversation.

Not everyone homeless lives in the streets. Some might be crashing on a friend's couch or living in their car.

Sometimes a person who is homeless doesn't need a place to sleep but desperately needs a kind word, a smile or a "Good morning," something that will encourage them to keep moving forward.

Offering a prayer of goodwill can be powerful to someone who is homeless. The right words from the Lord can make a big difference to someone who doesn't have their own home.

Many of us want to "help the poor" because of the good feeling it gives us. We are concerned about our consciences, not with whether our "help" has actually met their need.

True compassion gives people what they need, not just what they say they want. What many people need is not more money, but encouragement and hope. They need to know the Lord.

Remember that Jesus was also homeless! (Matthew 8:20 Jesus replied, *"Foxes have dens and birds have nests, but the Son of Man has no place to lay his head."*)

No matter what walk of life we come from, God loves us all the same. We all matter.

Have a blessed day and may the compassion of the Lord be with you.

DAY 7 – The Love of God is Powerful

> PSALM 103:11-12 *As high as the heavens are above the earth, so great is God's love for those who fear him. As far as the east is from the west, so far has he removed our transgressions from us.* NIV

As children of God, love is the basis of our whole identity, since love is what we were created to share with God and with each other. The love of God reaches farther than the stars. Our Lord is called the Most High for a reason. No love is more expansive.

When I became a Christian, I learned that God reaches beyond my mistakes, my fears, and my sins. If you can't imagine anything higher, remember God's love for you stretches farther that you can imagine.

God's love for us shows His favor without measure, though we often don't pay attention to Him. You can give love to those who don't deserve it because God gave you undeserved love, repeatedly, enduringly. Love is often expressed the most to those who deserve it the least.

When you stay in faith, you can overcome any obstacle and accomplish everything God has planned for you, even when change looks impossible.

Even when you've made poor choices and see no way out, God's hands are never tied. His power is unlimited. Nothing is too difficult for Him.

The love of God is powerful. Ask Him to fill you with the kind of love only He can provide. Then show love to others in a way that reflects your gratefulness to God for loving you. That, my friends, is the beauty and power of redeeming love.

Have a blessed day and may the love of the Lord be with you in everything you do.

DAY 8 – We All Matter

PROVERBS 22:2 *The rich and the poor have this in common: The Lord is the Maker of them all.* NKJV

No matter what walk of life you come from, we are all one in the sight of God. Jesus accepts all of us for who we are, no matter what our skin color, our financial situation or what we have done. He took our disease of sin upon himself and died in our place. Now, in God's eyes, we are all equal. We belong, we matter and we have been accepted. You are no longer an outcast. You are part of a huge family, God's family!

Everywhere you go, you are surrounded by people who were created by God, made with a purpose. Do you know what that means? It means that you matter; God has a unique plan for your life, as well as for every person.

The one true authority on your self-worth is Jesus Christ, and since He gave His own life up for us by dying on a cross, that should tell you just how valuable you really are! God will give you wisdom in all your struggles, as you seek the Truth that can only come from Him. My search for Truth has led me to Him and to the knowledge that I should accept people for who they are.

As I try to understand where others are coming from and let God work on their hearts, He gives me insight as to who a person is and how to attract them to Him. Don't try to change them. People will only change when they are ready and when God is at work in their lives. They have to want to change, which takes His help.

Understand that God does not play games. You know the games we play. God reveals His wisdom by His Spirit through His Word to those whose hearts are fully surrendered to Him.

Since we all matter, we should unite in God's love and strength as He is calling us to do, which will make an impact and a difference in our communities. Remember to be kind and loving to everyone because of what Jesus has done for us, and the great worth He places on us all.

Have a blessed day and may the peace of the Lord be with you as you seek His truth and His guidance and offer God's acceptance and love to every person, since everyone matters equally to Him.

DAY 9 – Putting God First

1 CORINTHIANS 10:31 *Therefore, whether you eat or drink, or whatever you do, do all to the glory of God.* NKJV

When it comes to our priorities, we consider what should be first, next and last. God says that He should be first, others second, and then yourself last.

So much for only looking out for #1, meaning yourself! Have you ever considered how much of your sin is centered on yourself? You want your own way, and you want to do life independent of God.

Satan's big sin was he considered himself greater than God. Do you consider yourself greater than God, or that God is unimportant?

The key to having God's abundant life—His love, peace and joy—is keeping Him in His rightful place in our priorities.

One of the first things I learned when I began to get serious about my relationship with the Lord is that He earnestly desires to be involved in every aspect of my life.

Each time we approach a problem, we have to remember that there's our way of doing it, and there's God's way. If we humbly and prayerfully give a problem or situation to God, He becomes responsible for seeing that it gets resolved. If we go ahead with it on our own, God is not obligated to direct our efforts, or to cause them to prosper. This is a recipe for frustration and failure for us.

Today I encourage you to put God first in your life. your life. Our relationship with God is the "cake" and anything else He blesses us with is the "icing."

Everyone have a blessed day and may the peace of the Lord be with you as you seek to bring Him glory in everything you do.

DAY 10 – God-given Passion

EPHESIANS 3:20 *Now to him who is able to do immeasurably more than all we ask or imagine, according to his power that is at work within us*. . . NIV

Passion is the God-given desire to make a difference, and it will energize you, making you more alive emotionally. This is God's way of moving you toward those people, roles, or causes that are His created agenda for your life. Find your passion and put it into ACTION. Passion makes our life worth living and gives us a purpose to live and die for.

Often we are busy "doing life," but not really enjoying it. Given the amount of time we spend working, failure to find meaningful, significant work is not just a minor misstep in living out God's plan, it's a deeper kind of failure that can make each day feel like living death. I believe our best gift to ourselves, our family, friends, and community is to find ways to express our hopes and dreams in our daily work. Work that integrates our gifts and passions, that is done for a worthy purpose, has always been a sign of maturity and wisdom.

We don't stop to think about what we were created to do.

Ask yourself what energizes you. Sometimes, we can't see our own gifts because we are so busy wanting everyone else's gift.

What are you passionate about? I mean really passionate about? Or put another way, what do you care about the most? Maybe it is a calling you've received, a dream you have, or a vision you've glimpsed.

Our hearts are hungry and we hunt all over for something (or someone) to fill the void that only He can fill. Over the years since He rescued me, God has shown me the source of my problem. I felt unmotivated because I didn't have God-given passion or purpose in my life! He helped me discern my passion.

What is *your* passion? If we all cared about the same things, many of the needs in this world would go unmet. We all have gifts that God has given us to use. He also gives us opportunities to serve in many areas: food outreach, children's ministry, youth ministry, homeless ministry, and prayer ministry.

I encourage you to identify your passion and purpose in God. Your passion may be for people, for a function or for a cause. Remember, we can't do this alone. God is calling us to be the hands and feet of Jesus. Have you put your passion into action?

Have a blessed day and may the peace of the Lord be with you as you find your passion and use it to serve others.

DAY 11 – You are Priceless to God

COLOSSIANS 3:16 *Let the message of Christ dwell among you richly.* NIV

We are all broken, whether we admit it or not.

Many think just because we help people in need that we are giving them a hand-out. I believe people are looking for encouragement, hope, faith, a kind word, a smile–something that will show them God cares. People are really looking for spiritual food, not just physical food.

We all need spiritual food. Without it, we can become spiritually bankrupt. That's why it's critical to read your Bible and find a church that encourages your walk with the Lord.

Many things are changing in our world. A lot of people are becoming more conscious and aware of issues and practices that have lasted for too long and must change in our society. Is God calling you to help with one of those issues?

Don't let the world define you. Are you tired of wearing a mask in order to be what others expect from you? You may search and question, trying to discover who you really are, while God is the answer to helping you discover the real you.

In order to help the broken, we must lead by example, by being spiritually healthy ourselves and respecting people for who they are and not for who we want them to be.

True strength comes from God. It's about having faith and trust in who God says you are, and a willingness to act upon it.

You might feel unwanted and unworthy to one person, but you are priceless to God. Don't ever forget your worth. The things that make you different are the things that make YOU, and the right people will love you for it. God does.

Have a blessed day and may the peace of the Lord be with you, as you understand how priceless you are to God.

DAY 12 – God is the Source of Wisdom

> PROVERBS 3:5-6 *Trust in the Lord with all your heart and lean not on your own understanding; in all your ways acknowledge him, and he shall direct your paths.* NKJV

A person can be very well-educated and full of knowledge but still lack wisdom. God is the source of wisdom for all things. Realize that He not only HAS the answer, He IS the answer.

Our trust in Him is supported by previous experiences in which we learned that God completely understands us, even with our present real issues needing resolution.

He wants to guide you to make free choices that enable you to better fulfill your purpose to become the best person He created you to be. Be intentionally involved in an on-going growth process that reflects your dignity and value as a person.

God does not make mistakes. When you take everything to God, you find everything you need. You see, God is hope for the hopeless, strength for the weak, love for those who feel unloved. Whatever you need, He has. God is really everything you want or need.

Every decision you make has consequences for good or bad. You have a choice to believe and fill your mind with God's truth, which will change your heart, or listen to what other people have to say.

Making a decision that is strongly influenced by God does not mean that it will be accompanied by ease or by fame. However, it is best to do what's right in God's eyes.

Sometimes, the hardest thing about making decisions is putting them into action, especially when it is the right thing to do.

Have a blessed day and may the peace of the Lord be with you, as you trust Him for wisdom.

DAY 13 – Let God Guide

> PSALM 48:14 *For that is what God is like. He is our God forever and ever, and he will guide us until we die.* NLT

So often we get far ahead of God because of our impatience. When we do that, we pay a big price for trying to move without God's direction.

We often make decisions on our own, do things without really praying about it, and do what we want to do without asking God. We can do that because He gave us free will.

However, I've realized that when I live my way, I will always make some major mistake which has consequences for which I will ultimately pay the price down the road.

My friends, this pertains to every aspect of life, including your family life, your relationships, your job, and what you do for recreation. Every part of your life is affected by your choices and your close daily fellowship with God abiding in Him. Let me encourage you today: Quit living your life your way. Why don't you let HIM guide you?

These two profound truths are in the Bible: 1) "Without me you can do nothing." 2) "You are to die to self." This means if you have given your life to Him, it's not your life anymore. It is HIS. Start letting God guide your decisions. It may not turn out exactly as you expected, but you will be surprised how much pain you avoid and how much better your life is when you live life His way and not your way.

He created you for His fellowship and service. You will be right where HE wants you, doing the things HE wants you to do.

Now my question is: "Isn't that where you really want to be?" Everyone have a blessed day. May the peace of the LORD be with you as you abide in Him and follow His guidance.

DAY 14 – Loving and Encouraging

> PROVERBS 4:7 *Getting wisdom is the wisest thing you can do! And whatever else you do, develop good judgement.* NLT

Spiritual growth is a part of the journey toward knowing not only who God created you to be, but who God is calling you to become.

My understanding of how to relate to others has focused on this single point: my role is not to convince or fix or save others — it's just to love them and let my love point them to the love of God.

God loves you whether you feel it or not! God has already provided everything you need to "win."

If you don't FEEL His love, it's not that God isn't giving it. Are you straining hard to earn His love that you already have? When you know you have something, it takes the struggle out of it. It removes doubt. How can you ever doubt that God has given you all you need? You already have it! It's really that simple.

Others tell me I have a gift of encouragement. I feel I have a calling to people who struggle with identity and acceptance – something I used to struggle with.

I try to offer unconditional acceptance and invite people into God's community. I want people to see themselves the way God sees them, so I try to offer affirmation and point to the beauty God placed in them.

My encouragement today is that in everything, set your eyes on God.

Have a blessed day and may the peace of the Lord be with you as you love and encourage others.

DAY 15 – Misplaced Expectations

> JOHN 8:12 *Jesus spoke to the people once more and said, "I am the light of the world. If you follow me, you won't have to walk in darkness, because you will have the light that leads to life."* NIV

Most people follow what they think is their own plan when they are really just living for the approval of others.

Our biggest disappointments are often the result of misplaced expectations. This is especially true when it comes to our relationships and interactions with others.

You are not in this world to live up to the expectations of others, nor should you feel that others are here to live up to yours. In fact, the more God guides your decisions in life, the less approval you will need from everyone else.

God gives you a new chance every day. The fact that God gave you life should be the motivation to start aligning your priorities based on what is the best reflection of who you are as a child of God, instead of some hollow path based on expectations and opinions of other people.

God is saying, "Follow me and see your old ways mended."

You have to learn to follow what God has placed in your heart. You can't let other people pressure you into being something that you're not. If you want God's favor in your life, you must be the person He made you to be, not the person others want you to be. Don't let outside expectations keep you from following the path God has for you.

Life is completely (and only) what you make it, with God's guidance. Your perception is what you decide it is. God has given you the power to see life through His eyes. Follow Him.

Have a blessed day and may the peace of the Lord be with you, as you walk in His light and let go of others' expectations.

DAY 16 – Spiritual Beauty

> 1 SAMUEL 16:7 *But the Lord said to Samuel, "Do not consider his appearance or his height, for I have rejected him. The Lord does not look at the things man looks at. Man looks at the outward appearance, but the Lord looks at the heart."* NLT

Unfortunately, we live in a superficial world where people judge on appearance. We would all love to say that we are not in the majority, and that we all look beyond what's on the outside, but virtually all of us are influenced by appearance.

What is beautiful in God's eyes? Recognizing the qualities God has cherished in the lives of other people is one way to determine His concept of beauty. In I Samuel, God looked at David's heart.

An awareness of one's spiritual poverty, sorrow for wickedness, hunger and thirst for righteousness, mercy, purity of heart, and being a peacemaker are all qualities of beauty to God.

However, just as a beautiful appearance can become ugly through neglect, a beautiful life of righteousness can become ugly through neglect of our inner spiritual walk with God.

Spiritual beauty must never be taken for granted or be neglected. Remember that just as it is possible to be one of society's most impressive people but be ugly in God's eyes, it is also possible to be an unknown in society and to be radiantly beautiful in His eyes.

God looks at your heart!

Have a blessed day and may the peace of the Lord be with you, as you understand God's standard of spiritual beauty.

DAY 17 – Remain Committed to the Lord

PROVERBS 16:3 *Commit to the Lord whatever you do, and he will establish your plans.* NIV

Today's world has programmed us to expect a life of ease. It's not merely that we want everything to be easy; who wouldn't want that?

What is crazy is that we now expect to receive abundant rewards with minimal effort. If something requires effort or time, we think it must not be meant to happen, and we feel thoroughly justified giving up.

Some of the best things in life demand effort and prove worthy of whatever amount of labor we endure in that pursuit.

Even our spiritual growth is reflective of our faithful investment. We don't want to hear it, but following God involves sacrifice, effort, devotion, but His rewards are amazing!

Effective leadership flows from being deeply committed to the right things, whether in our home or our jobs. As children of God, the single most important commitment of our lives is, obviously, to God, then spouse and family. Any lasting success we experience as leaders will flow from that commitment to do the next right thing in the next right way, as God directs.

Quality relationships are founded on the Rock of God and commitment to Him. To live without such commitment is to live in the darkness that knows neither victory nor defeat.

As children of God, we are called to remain committed to Him, even when we don't fully understand all of His plans for us.

Have a blessed day and may the peace of the Lord be with you as you commit your way to Him.

DAY 18 – Hope

PSALM 43:5 *Why am I so sad? Why am I so troubled? I will put my hope in God, and once again I will praise him, my savior and my God.* GNT

There is no medicine like hope; no incentive so great and no tonic so powerful as an expectation of a better tomorrow. Hope keeps us alive and moving forward, no matter what happens.

Always be hopeful because your hope is placed in God, not in circumstances or other people. Always have something to look forward to. Believe that tomorrow holds something better for you. No matter what your situation, or what you're going through right now, never lose hope.

Even in the midst of our struggles, where it seems there is no way out, God's Word reminds us that with Him, there is always hope.

Our identity is found in Jesus Christ. It is this truth that gives us unconditional love, security and hope. It is not based on our identity, but on what God has already accomplished at the cross of Jesus Christ.

Maybe you feel hopeless today. Maybe you are in a dark place, overwhelmed by the situations you are facing and wondering if and when it will ever get better.

In times like these I encourage you to go to the Lord, and I promise He will give you what you need. If it is peace, He will give His peace. If it is comfort, He will comfort. If it is guidance, He will guide you. If it is hope, He will give you hope. Seek His heart, and He will give you what you need – and what you truly want.

Have a blessed day and may the hope of the Lord be with you, as you trust in Him and encourage others to do so, as well.

DAY 19 – Focus on Today, Not the Quicksand of the Past

PHILIPPIANS 4:12 *I know what it is to be in need, and I know what it is to have plenty. I have learned the secret of being content in any and every situation, whether well fed or hungry, whether living in plenty or in want.* NIV

Do you wake up some days and just don't feel like fighting any longer? Are you tired of the battles, tired of the struggles with no desire to keep going?

How often are you weary and tired because you are still looking back, allowing the problems and situations of the past to hold you down?

I have learned that what's in the past is done and gone. The enemy wants to hold you back by keeping you focused on the past. Let it go and live today.

Focus on today and tomorrow, not yesterday. It's time to turn everything over to God and start living today, whatever your problems are. Most of your circumstances aren't going to be fixed quickly, aren't going to have an overnight answer, and it's going to take a power much greater than you to repair. After all, if you could fix it yourself, you would have already done it.

Turn it over to God. Does that make it go away magically? No, but it does put it in the hands of the Lord who can and will start working it through and getting you beyond those circumstances.

You have today in front of you. Get out of the quicksand of the past and start living for Him today. You will be surprised how much quicker and easier your past problems will straighten out.

Have a blessed day and may the peace of the Lord be with you, as you focus on today and release the past to Him.

DAY 20 – Love

> ROMANS 12:10 *Love each other with genuine affection, and take delight in honoring each other.* NLT

> EPHESIANS 4:2 *Be completely humble and gentle; be patient, bearing with one another in love.* NIV

Love bears the storms of disappointment, the rains of failure and the winds of time and circumstances.

Love shields from the extremes of this cruel world.

Love provides a place of shelter that can withstand the worst situations imaginable.

Love does not insulate us from the harsh realities of living in a broken world. Neither can it protect us from consequences of our own choices. But love does give broken, hurting people a place to find the Someone who truly cares from His heart for their welfare.

Love gives even unrepentant people an advocate and intercessor who prays for their ultimate well-being.

Bearing with one another does not mean that we should be a doormat and let everyone step on us. It means that love never stops caring and never stops offering a place of forgiveness, even if the other person continues to do the same wrong thing.

Love never gets to the point where it begins hating, despising or judging. Love cares enough to keep praying, to patiently endure the sins of others, to confront when necessary and to forgive. This is all possible because God first loved us, enabling us to love. (*We love because God first loved us.* I John 4:19 GNT)

1 John 4:8 tells us that *God is love*. While love's character never changes, its strategies and tactics constantly adapt to seek the well-being of the other person in all things.

Have a blessed day and may the love of the Lord be with you.

DAY 21 – Guard Your Mind; You Will Reap What You Sow

> GALATIANS 6:7 *Do not be deceived: God cannot be mocked. A man reaps what he sows.* NIV

> PROVERBS 4:23 *Guard your heart above all else, for it determines the course of your life.* NLT

The mind is like a farm. If a farmer plants corn he will get corn. If he plants wheat, he will get wheat. It would be impossible for the farmer to plant corn and expect to harvest wheat. It is simple; whatever you plant is what you will get.

For instance, a person who sows a life of crime can expect to reap prison. A person who sows hard work and commitment to her job, in turn, reaps a promotion.

If you sow to the flesh, you will reap corruption. It is impossible for you to sow to yourself and get a spiritual harvest. God has given you the ability to control what you sow and thereby control what you harvest.

If you experience defeat because of sin, lack power, and never really walk in all the fullness of God, then it is time to examine your thoughts and heart.

God has made you fully responsible for what you sow. God has created you in such a way that your actions follow your thoughts. Many assume that thoughts are not all that important as long as you're able to follow a prescribed set of "do's and don'ts" in outward conduct.

The person who believes either of these assumptions is only fooling himself. Failing to come to grips with this issue leads to an empty, unstable life, never to victorious and joyous living.

Your attitudes and behavior are but a reflection of what goes into your mind! You cannot experience the fullness of God if you continue to hold wrong desires and beliefs in your heart. Once you have let God remove them from your heart, you must "guard your heart above all else" (Proverbs 4:23) to prevent more wrong desires or beliefs from creeping back into your heart and mind.

Your mind cannot be renewed on a starvation diet. Take heed to your thought life. Stop thinking about what doesn't need to be entertained! Spend time in God's Word and communicating with Him.

As you go about making your life choices and decisions, realize that God cannot be mocked. At some point, there will be significant consequences when you do that which is wrong.

On the flip side, when you do that which is right, you can expect to reap blessings in your life. Try to do the right things, and then be confident that, in due time, God will allow you to reap a harvest from the good seeds you have sown. The question is: What kind of seed are you sowing?

Have a blessed day and may the peace of the Lord be with you, as you make life choices to sow the right kind of seed – all with His help and guidance.

DAY 22 – Baby Steps of Faith to Serve Others

JOHN 15:16 *You didn't choose me. I chose you.
I appointed you to go and produce lasting fruit,
so that the Father will give you whatever you ask
for, using my name.* NLT

Baby steps of faith led me to a place where God inspired me to do what I do.

When we surrender our life to God and ask Him to show us what He wants us to do, He will give us the ability to get it done.

We are all born with little tiny seeds of inspiration inside of us. It's why we all have unique talents, likes, interests, and passions. However, as we grow into adults, we often lose connection to this inspiration. Caught up in the responsibility of daily lives, our passion and true desires often get put on hold. Instead of chasing and forcing, we can find the answers we desire in stillness and listening to God.

Passion presents itself in many different forms. Begin by giving of yourself. Serving others makes our time here on earth more fulfilling and meaningful, whether it's helping out a neighbor or fellow church member or volunteering at a soup kitchen. Even if you can't give money, giving of your time can be a blessing to others. While service to people who are homeless begins with an individual commitment to Jesus' call for compassion and justice, it is within the community of believers that this work can be truly effective. Our Lord takes personally how we treat the poor.

While shoveling money and goods at poor people may help us – and them – feel good for the short run, it takes more thought, time and commitment on our part and theirs, to help them do what is best in the long run. We cannot relate meaningfully to the poor when we are isolated from them.

For some of us it's a question of walking down the block and getting to know the poor. For others it's driving twenty miles to find a homeless person. Caring for the poor is a sobering responsibility for which we will all be held accountable.

Today I encourage you to keep the big vision always in your heart, but keep the daily focus on the placement of each stone or baby step needed to create that vision. God will guide you.

Have a blessed day and may the peace of the Lord be with you as you take baby steps of faith and serve others.

DAY 23 – Respect

MATTHEW 7:12 *Do to others whatever you would like them to do to you. This is the essence of all that is taught in the law and the prophets.* NIV

We all desire relationships in which we are accepted, valued, respected and wanted. Being respected and valued is a great feeling! Having respect means treating yourself and others with kindness and consideration. It means taking care of yourself and being aware of how your actions affect others.

Respect is like a boomerang. If you throw respect out at the world, it will come right back to you. If you do not respect yourself or others, no one else will respect you either.

Giving respect to others means valuing them and their thoughts and feelings. It also means acknowledging them, listening to them, being truthful with them, and accepting them and their differences.

So, how do we respect others? Simply follow the "Golden Rule": *Do unto others, as you would have them do unto you.* If you do not want anyone to call you names, then do not call anyone names and accept those who are different from you.

Don't worry about being affirmed, being right, demanding respect, judging others, keeping score, harboring bitterness, competing, gossiping, or bickering. Be more concerned that you are giving respect and showing the love of God to others. Remember that no one is better than you, and you are no better than anyone else.

If this is hard, then ask God to help you to treat others – and yourself – with respect.

Have a blessed day and may the peace of the Lord be with you, as you respect yourself and others.

DAY 24 – The Joy of the Lord

PSALMS 100:2 *Serve the Lord with gladness; come before Him with joyful songs.* HCSB

The joy of God is deep down within, continuous and encompasses your whole being.

Do you ever get so wrapped up in your day-to-day issues and activities that you often take God's blessings for granted? Despite problems in your life today, there is a joy that can get you beyond those problems.

Don't get caught up in the everyday foolishness and lose sight of why you are here. If your life is focused on your relationship with the Lord and your service to Him, and you are involved in helping others each day, then not only are you fulfilling your purpose, but you will enjoy the blessings of peace, joy and abundance from the Lord.

God is offering His joy to you. Pray and ask Him to open your heart, help you through the difficulties and put HIS joy in your life today, regardless of your circumstances.

Trust me, having the joy of the Lord can give you the strength you need to overcome and be victorious in any situation, even cancer.

At one time it was impossible for me to understand the concept of Godly joy in the face of so many problems. But today the joy I experience comes from my desire to serve Him, knowing that God is working on my behalf. He is working on your behalf, too.

His joy is not for sale, but free to those who ask for it. Anything that you ask for in His name, with His heart and perspective, shall be given to you. What's stopping you?

Have a blessed day and may the joy of the Lord be with you.

DAY 25 – Give God Your Problems

1 PETER 5:7 *Cast all your anxiety on him because he cares for you.* NIV

For many of us the concerns we are facing have been problems for a while. We give them to God; then we take them back.

Despite all of the praying and worrying, we still have the same problems. Then we begin to wonder if anyone is listening or really cares about what we are facing.

Let me encourage you today. The Bible proclaims that God not only hears our prayers, but He answers them, as well.

God allows things to happen at exactly the right time! Our job is not to figure out when, but to make up our mind that we won't give up until we cross the finish line. The more we trust God and keep our eyes focused on Him, the more abundant life we will have. It is His good pleasure to bless his children.

We have His precious promise to cast our cares on Him. No matter what your mind may tell you, your faith has to step in and assure you that God is hearing your prayers.

No matter how you may feel, when all others abandon or mistreat you, God is always there. He is there to love you, hold you, and comfort you.

Do not let the problems you have today ever let you think that God doesn't care. Start today to believe with confidence and assurance that GOD LOVES YOU. And that He will never leave you nor forsake you.

Trusting God brings life. Believing brings rest.

Have a blessed day and may the peace of the Lord be with you, as you give all your anxiety to Him.

DAY 26 – Trust God Daily

ROMANS 8:28 *And we know that all things work together for good to those who love God, to those who are called according to His purpose.* NKJV

God will sometimes allow trials and tests. In spite of pain, suffering, or rejection, we must never doubt that God loves us, is in control and has a plan which He is going to work out for our ultimate good.

It is vital that we surrender all to Him and let Him deliver us and heal our wounds and guide us. He will shape us into useful instruments for His purposes.

Everyone has tried to get God to approve their own definition of right and wrong, but God never changes, and His standards never change.

I don't know what your story is, but I encourage you to trust God even when you don't understand what's happening in your life. God will give you peace as you learn to step out in faith and trust Him, even when you don't understand.

You must decide whether to live your life according to personal preference or according to the unchanging Word of God. You may not understand how God is causing *all things to work together for good* (Romans 8:28), but when we *trust Him with all our hearts* (Proverbs 3:5-6), we know that He is working things out for our long-term good. He will never fail us.

I encourage you to open your heart to the Lord and seek His face today. Ask Him to help you walk by faith not by sight, no matter what you are going through. His peace is not temporary.

Have a blessed day and may the peace of the Lord be permanently with you as you open your heart and trust Him daily.

DAY 27 – Humility

ROMAN'S 13:4 *For the one in authority is God's servant for your good. But if you do wrong, be afraid, for rulers do not bear the sword for no reason. They are God's servants, agents of wrath to bring punishment on the wrongdoer.* NIV

When we disagree with someone, humility is our greatest response. The moment we justify or defend ourselves before another, we yield to their judgment instead of God's.

I've learned that humility ushers in God's grace, which is His empowerment and a mighty weapon against the people who always find pleasure in doing wrong to others.

In a world that cries out for quick results and convenient answers, it is hard to have an attitude of steadfast humility. The temptation is always to defend ourselves, even when doing so leads to strife.

But when we humble ourselves by obeying God's Word, then His favor, grace, and righteous judgment rest upon us. He will, without any doubt, bring the situation to resolution at just the right time – His time, not ours.

We can't pick and choose when we want His guidance. It's interesting that we don't ask for God's input on every decision; we only seem to want His input when it's convenient to us. God wants 100% in this relationship, not 50%.

Are we doing right in our eyes or in God's eyes? The Bible says in Judges 17:6 *Everyone did what was right in his own eyes.* (ESV) We're not talking about people who chose to do wrong. They chose to do right; but they CHOSE FOR THEMSELVES what was right. These are people who said, "I want to do right, but I will decide what's right." Something to think about!!!

Have a blessed day and may the peace of the Lord be with you as you wait humbly for God's perfect timing.

DAY 28 – Wearing a Mask

> 2 TIMOTHY 2:15 *Do your best to win full approval in God's sight, as a worker who is not ashamed of his work, one who correctly teaches the message of God's truth.* GNT

Do you say you are Godly, but your actions say something different? Do you say that you've changed, but deep inside you still do the same old things? You say you love and you care, but do you really? The lips can say so much, but what does your heart say? Your thoughts and words are coming from your heart.

You can have secrets and wear a mask that hides who you really are and how you're really feeling. We are taught by society to hide our true feelings and thoughts, and conform to others' ways of thinking, which masks our true selves. Take off any masks that give a dishonest appearance to others.

As our own eyes are opened more and more, we ultimately wonder how we remained blind for so long. It is quite easy to gradually slip back into the darkness again, especially when we have so much foolishness around us.

We may call Jesus our Lord when we stand before him; yet He has warned us that calling Him Lord is not enough. (Matthew 7:21 *Not everyone who says to me, 'Lord, Lord,' will enter the kingdom of heaven, but the one who does the will of my Father who is in heaven.* ESV) Our faith must be proved genuine by devoted obedience to Him.

The problem with wearing masks is that we end up losing our integrity, because we're not being honest with others or ourselves about who we really are. God sees behind our mask no matter how many times we change it. Still He chooses to love us.

Have a blessed day and may the peace of the Lord be with you as you choose to be vulnerable and drop any masks.

DAY 29 – God is with Us in Our Struggle to Forgive

JOSHUA 1:9 *Have I not commanded you? Be strong and courageous. Do not be afraid; do not be discouraged, for the Lord your God will be with you wherever you go."* NIV

Jesus experienced temptation, loss, persecution and suffering. He never promised that life would be easy for us, but He promised to help us when we struggle. Struggles of life are part of our story.

Many people struggle with forgiveness. Often, they either are unable to forgive or they forgive too quickly without fully processing their emotions or resolving the situation.

We each have to decide to let go of the past in order to grow and make room for something better. Sometimes our self-protection harms us and stifles the capacity for us to be open and experience joy, love, and peace.

When it comes to trusting each other, we have to accept that our past is not our present. We must recognize that what hurt us before is not necessarily what is currently standing before us— even sometimes when the situation looks similar or the cause is the same person.

Letting go is the greatest act of love for ourself and others. In love and in life, our vulnerability is one of our greatest strengths. We often believe that we risk too much by being vulnerable, but, in fact, the opposite is true. When we build a wall around us to protect ourselves from our big, bad fears, we miss out on so much.

When we live with the mindset that something may be taken from us (physically or emotionally), or that we need to be in control of everything that happens, we endure fear on a daily basis.

It's exhausting to live that way. It makes us cynical, suspicious, and unable to follow our hearts because we are afraid of what might happen. It stops us from following God.

We have to choose to forgive those who don't believe in us or have hurt us in any way, and keep moving forward. Don't give up. God believes in you. When we lose trust and betray God in our thinking, doesn't He forgive us? Of course He does!

Have a blessed day and may the forgiveness of the Lord be with you as you also forgive others – whether they "deserve" it or not.

DAY 30 – Let God's Light Shine in Your Heart

> ISAIAH 9:2 *The people who are now living in darkness will see a great light. They are now living in a very dark land. But a light will shine on them.* NIRV

Deep down within each of us there's a place that is made for one thing—a relationship with God. No matter how hard we try to cover it up or fill it with something else, we will never be satisfied. Our hearts will remain restless until they find their home with God. That deep, hidden part of us is there, even if we haven't realized it until now.

Even though we make mistakes, God doesn't leave us. In His kindness and mercy, He sustains us—blessing us even when we don't know it, so we can eventually find our way to Him.

But if we don't seek Him and His ways, or if we choose to reject Him, our spiritual deaths will be permanent. We will live apart from God and His goodness in eternity after we physically die.

The Bible tells us that eternal life apart from God is to live in darkness forever, with no hope, no joy, and no love. God knew that we needed to be rescued. He loved us so much that He devised a plan to free us from all the hurts, habits and hang-ups and provide forgiveness for all time.

God is love. He loves you more than anyone else ever has or ever could. In giving your life to Him, you invite His love into every aspect of who you are. His love is transforming, and His forgiveness is complete. God will transform you and make you a new person in Him. You will find the joy-filled life you've always

135

longed to have. The will of God will never take you to where the grace of God will not protect you!

Have a blessed day and may the peace of the Lord be with you, as you allow God to shine His light in your heart.

For more information on Victor Newman Ministries, or for an update on Yvette, visit our website:

http://www.VictorNewman.org/, or follow us on Facebook.

CPSIA information can be obtained
at www.ICGtesting.com
Printed in the USA
LVHW020839250219
608648LV00021B/198/P